TECHNOLO

A Systems Approach

John Myerson

Stanley Thornes (Publishers) Ltd

First published in 1990 by:
Stanley Thornes (Publishers) Ltd
Old Station Drive
Leckhampton
CHELTENHAM GL53 0DN
England

British Library Cataloguing in Publication Data

Myerson, John
Technology: a systems approach
    1. Technology
    I. Title
    600

    ISBN 0 7487 0201 6

Design by Ron Kamen

Typeset by Microset Graphics Ltd, Basingstoke

Printed in Great Britain at The Bath Press, Avon

Illustrations by Claire James and Tek Art

Produced by AMR

CONTENTS

*See colour section

3

Acknowledgements

My thanks to the staff and pupils in CDT departments of schools in the London Borough of Richmond for their help and encouragement with this book, and to Mr P. J. Lomax, Inspector for CDT, for writing the Introduction. My thanks also to the British Standards Institution for permission to reproduce some of their symbols and to Eileen Jarvis for her excellent efforts in editing this work.

Grateful thanks to the following for allowing their photographs to be used:

G. Alexander/Cabaret Mechanical Theatre, Covent Garden p39; Central Electricity Generating Board p9, p18, p22; Docklands Light Railway Ltd p11; Roland Emmett p7; Intermediate Technology Development Group p8, p48, p91; K. L. Jeenay plc p75; Patrick Johns p10; London Underground Ltd p35; City of Newcastle upon Tyne, City Engineer's Photo Unit p23; The High Commissioner for New Zealand p24; Barry Page p22; A. B. Pharos Marine Ltd p49; Power Propellor Co Ltd p70; Rex Features *(The Independent)* p74; Sarah Saunders p7, p17; UK Atomic Energy Authority p21; Timothy Williams p53.

   All other photographs are by the author.

Every effort has been made to contact copyright holders but we apologise if any have been overlooked.

Preface

The systems approach has been adopted in order to cover the main principles of Technology as a framework for design and project work, without relying on excessive amounts of factual knowledge.

The recent report of the National Curriculum Working Party for Design and Technology has emphasised the importance of the process of designing, making and evaluating in the development of technological capability. The contexts in which this process is active are many and varied, according to pupils' interests and abilities. Often the amount of detailed knowledge of particular technologies is determined by the choice of problem to be tackled.

The systems approach is particularly based on the CDT: Technology syllabuses developed by the Northern Examining Association and the Scottish Curriculum Development Service, but the National Criteria for CDT and all other GCSE Technology syllabuses endorse the systems approach in that the outcomes from technological work can be either artefacts or systems.

Almost all GCSE syllabuses in CDT assume that there has been continuous progress in design and technological experience from an early age. This book has been designed to make use of such experience in Primary and Lower Secondary Schools and provide the methodology and minimum knowledge base to stimulate and interest a wide range of pupils.

John Myerson, 1990

INTRODUCTION

What is it?

Technology influences all of our lives. There is hardly anything around us which is not affected by technological development. When we talk of living in a technological age, we are referring to a rapidly growing and readily available advanced technology, and we all use it to a greater or lesser degree. The word **technology**, as in common use, describes the things or products of our modern society. However, these are but the results of human endeavour and the complex organisation of society which has developed alongside technological advance. *Technology is an interaction of knowledge, skill and social organisation.*

Advance in technology is only possible if society is sufficiently developed to support it. Society must provide a skilled labour force, education and training, transport and communication systems, and locally available energy and resources. But, to help people overcome their own problems, the technology must be appropriate and compatible with their own culture and economic conditions.

New technology has a considerable influence on society. Increased work capacity through the use of machines and tools significantly changes the pattern of both work and leisure time. The benefits of new technology reach us all: from computerised check-out at the supermarket to improved medical care and monitoring in hospitals.

Technology is also a social process. It is a way of achieving things: of inventing and planning to overcome specific problems.

The word technology is from the Greek *tekhnologia*:

  tekhne ... an art or skill;
  logia ... an area of knowledge or study.

So it means the study of an art or skill. The process of technology is to produce something, be it a component or a set of components in a system.

Its development

People first became technologists when they learned to take advantage of the materials and natural happenings of the physical world. Using sticks, bones and stones as tools, people tried to provide for their basic needs: food and shelter.

The food supply relied upon, and the resources available greatly influenced the possible solutions to meeting the need for shelter.

▲ *Permanent housing?*

Portable housing? ▶

Better housing and plentiful food supplies provide the conditions for population growth.

The development of technology enables us to exercise control over our environment. Through planning and the development of tools we extend our capabilities. We develop machines such as the lever and the pulley to aid human muscles. We harness energy to overcome our own limited work rate. From harnessing the horse, we have gone on to harness the wind, water, fossil fuels and nuclear power. We have improved our ability to control through electronics, pneumatics and servomechanics. The capability of the human brain is extended through computers and microelectronic devices.

Its process

Design is a technological process. We design things and systems to meet people's needs. If we are to design things well we must understand both the needs and problems and the society in which they arise. This is the heart of technology.

Needs may be basic and obvious like food, shelter and a comfortable environment. Other needs arise from our way of life. If we look closely at almost any aspect of our community there are plenty of problems to be tackled, such as help for the elderly and infirm, improvement to 'rush hour' transport and the provision of housing. There are also social and psychological needs like aesthetic pleasure and self esteem and these should not be forgotten.

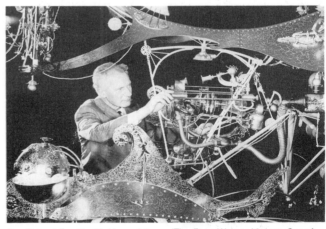

▲ *Roland Emett with his sculpture: 'The Borg-Warner Vintage Car of the Future'*

There will always be a need for technologists. As time progresses, knowledge increases and technology develops improved solutions will be found to the existing problems.

Technology is about knowing **what** is wanted, and **why** it is wanted, and then working out **how** to achieve it with what is available.

P. Lomax

SYSTEMS

What is a system?

A one-way system

To make things happen in the world, people and materials need to be organised to work together. For example, people can be organised in an education system, or have a collection of hardware in their home which is arranged as a central-heating system. Most of us will have been driven around a one-way system, hopefully the right way!

All these examples, and there are many others, use the word **system** in their name. Almost any organisation or orderly set of parts can be described as a system.

The main advantage of a **systems approach** is that we can look at the broad outline of a problem without having to consider complex details or any particular technology.

An everyday problem

▲ Washing clothes in a river

Washing clothes can be a problem for any type of society. Some have had to solve it by simply bashing the clothes on rocks at a river's edge. This wears the clothes out rather quickly and requires human time and effort!

A systems approach to this problem would first need to decide what the complete system would have to do. This could be to: receive dirty clothes, sort, wash, rinse, dry, iron and then deliver the clean clothes. An understanding of how dirt is trapped in clothing fibres and how it could be dislodged would be important before deciding on the exact nature of the process.

The result of analysing a complete system like this could be the design of an automatic washer/dryer for home use, or the organisation of a 'production line' laundry with several employees and collection/delivery vans, or even a fully automated cleaning factory. The processes involved and the final results may be similar, but the scale of operation is completely different. There is certainly plenty of scope for further design work on this system, particularly in the processes, and possibly even for the development of clothing that does not get dirty!

Did you know?

In the 1860s people were using wooden boxes turned by a handle to 'tumble wash' their clothes. By 1914, rotating wooden boxes were driven by electric motors and these made rather dangerous washing 'machines'!

In the example above, and in all systems, the desired result or **output** can be identified. The **input** or inputs to the system are not always so obvious but must be present, and some form of **process** or response to the input is needed to give the desired result.

Most systems will also need an **energy** input to keep the process going, unless the system input is a form of energy or the system is an energy converter. All systems will also need a method of **control**, if only to simply switch the process on and off.

A bicycle dynamo is an example of an **energy converter**. For the type shown in the illustration, the input is controlled by moving the dynamo's friction wheel away from the tyre. The hub type of dynamo is constantly generating electricity while the wheel is rotating. In this case it is the output which can be switched on or off as a control.

Often systems are controlled by the amount of energy reaching the process. Control methods are looked at in more detail on page 25.

▲ *Bicycle dynamo*

rotary motion of **magnet in coil** produces **6 volts AC**

Breakdown

Technology is not perfect! Systems sometimes stop working and need closer inspection or **trouble-shooting**. In the design process, systems can be 'broken-down' in a different sense, into smaller units or **subsystems**, so that the function of the whole can be understood.

There are two ways to analyse systems into subsystems:

1   Divide up the main process into a **chain** of smaller processes each having its own input and output. The output of the first **subprocess** becomes the input of the second subprocess, and so on to the final output.

▲ *Power station*

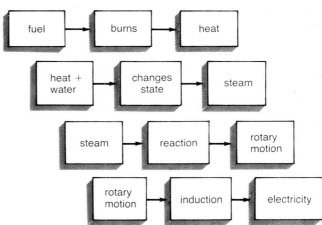

▲ *Subprocesses*

2   Look at the whole system and identify the various **functions** which together make the system work. Then decide the input, process and output for each function, separately.

FUNCTIONS OF A WINDMILL:	
lift grain sacks	spill wind if too strong
direct grain onto stones	direct flour into sacks
turn sails into wind	stop sails turning
grind grain into flour	lower sacks to ground
regulate speed of stones	

SYSTEMS

Designing systems

Decisions to be made
1 Output wanted
2 Input available
3 How to do it?

1 What do you want your system to do?
What problem are you trying to solve?
What is the final result?
In what form is your intended output?

Control of temperature in greenhouse

In order to keep plants through a British winter it is often necessary to provide some form of heating in a greenhouse. (The problem of heat loss is looked at on page 20.)

Basic system:

| TEMPERATURE | → | a process | → | HEAT |

1 Output desired: heat to raise air temperature.

Form of output	Comment on suitability
Electrical resistance heater	Easy to switch on and off, but wiring may be difficult in garden.
Solid fuel heater	Cannot easily be switched on and off. Needs to be refilled by hand.
Oil or gas heater	Fairly easy to control needs pipeline from tank or mains.

2 What type of input can you use?
What will start the system going?
Will the input be movement, heat energy, an electrical signal, light, sound, or perhaps materials?

2 The input to the system is a particular value of temperature which only depends on the type of plants being grown and will be determined by the weather outside.

3 Now, find a number of possible processes which will change your chosen input into the desired output. It is often helpful to look for a subsystem which will change the input into something more easily processed, as in the example.

3

Process possibilities	Comment on suitability
Mercury thermometer	Would have to be read by user and heater switched on manually. Possibly could be read by light sensor?
Thermostat (bimetal strip)	Direct switching of heater, but has fairly slow response to change in temperature.
Thermistor	Would need electronics to convert signal, but has much faster response.

Activity

Analyse a project you have already done using the systems approach as on page 9. What output did you need? What input did you supply? What process did you use?

The Docklands Light Railway

An example of a transport system design

ROUTE MAP

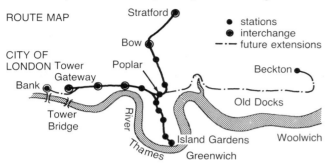

The need

The London docklands were built between 1800 and 1921, but because of bomb damage during World War II and changes in the handling of cargo, the docks began to close down in 1967. The decline of the docks and the resulting reduction in local employment caused a drop in demand for public transport in the area.

When the decision was taken to rebuild the area it was realised that a new public transport system would be required to encourage commercial and residential development.

▲ A Docklands train at West India Quay Station

▲ DLR Control Room. On left, power supplies/control and radio; lower centre, train supervision and control; upper centre, television monitors of station platforms.

▲ DLR Ticket issuing machines

Possible solutions

The initial plan was for an extension of the Underground railway, mainly in tunnels, but the cost was estimated then to be over £325 million and the finance was not available.

It was also considered that a bus service would not be able to cope with the levels of traffic which would eventually use the system.

The final and accepted proposal was to build a Light Rapid Transit system because such small, lightweight vehicles could handle steeper gradients and tighter curves than conventional trains. Construction would be easier because less land would be required and bridges could be lighter structures. Extensive use could be made of existing disused railway routes. The scheme was completed in July 1987.

Other design considerations

The Railway has been designed as an **integrated system** with special attention being given to ease of passenger use and low operation costs.

Because of the compact nature of the routes, trains are controlled automatically from a Control Centre at Poplar, but each train is staffed for safety and for the reassurance of passengers. In order to monitor the use of stations the Control Centre is provided with closed circuit television cameras and video recorders. Passengers can speak to the Controller by microphone in emergencies such as track power failure.

Much of the line is above ground level and lifts are provided for disabled users. The platform edges are straight and level with the train floors and there is a maximum 75 mm gap for ease of wheelchair access.

Tickets are available from local newsagents or from vending machines. There are no staff at station stops. These are similar to bus stops and are provided with a simple shelter and train destination indicator.

SYSTEMS

Development of a system

To illustrate the development of a complete system from a **brief**, a number of stages in the design have been selected. It must be emphasised that there are other possible solutions to this brief (such as the use of pneumatics) and other ways of looking at the stages in designing. The detailed choice of components is not done until the complete system has been thought out.

The Brief: To enable a person to open his or her garage door from the outside without leaving the car.

Stage One

Problem: Mechanical linkage to door needs to be driven remotely.

Stage Two

Possible solution: Use an electric motor.

Problem: If there is only one sensor, could the door be easily opened by unauthorised persons?

Stage Three

Possible solution: Add extra (and possibly different) sensors which can *only* give an input together, e.g. light from headlamps *and* sound of horn.

Problem: Electric motor will only stay on while sensors are giving an input. It needs to stay on while the door is opening.

Stage Four

Possible solution: Add a **latch** to keep the motor on even if sensors are not giving an input.

Problem: Door is fully open and the motor must be switched off!

Stage Five

Possible solution: Add a **limit switch** operated by the mechanism when the door is fully open.

Problem: Door needs to be closed after car has been driven in.

Stage Six

Possible solution: Reverse the direction of rotation of the electric motor by switching.

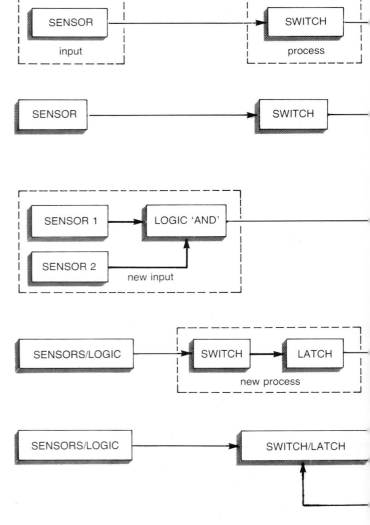

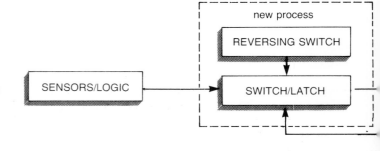

Decisions need to be made about the details such as:
- the types of sensors and their positions   (see pages 89, 90)
- the method of logic used   (see page 32)
- a suitable switch unit, e.g. transistor switch   (see page 59)
- a latching method, e.g. a relay   (see page 30)
- the type of electric motor and mechanism
- the position of the limit switch (or switches).

A first complete design needs to be tested using a **fast modelling method**. In fact, if you have access to a **systems electronics kit**, the stages above can be modelled and tested as you think about the design. When the function of the system is satisfactory a **prototype** can be built and attention given to the position of wiring, the protection of circuitry and the 'look' of the finished devices.

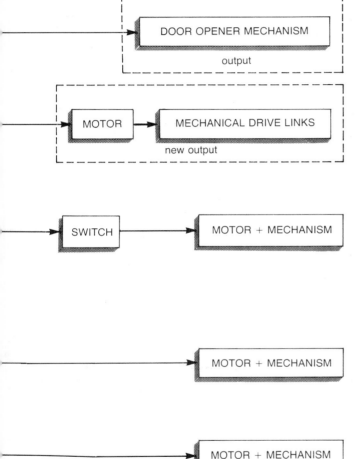

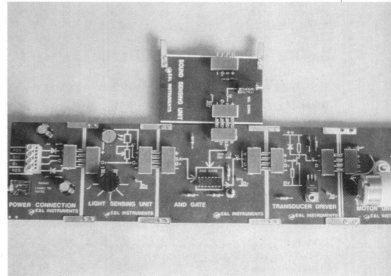

▲   A systems electronics kit

Activity

Develop a system from the given brief using block diagrams such as in the example.

Brief: To enable animals to live in a healthy environment, where temperature, light, water and food supply, and exercise, are all carefully controlled.

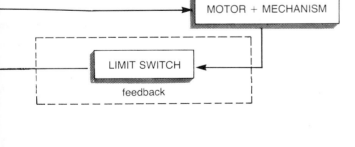

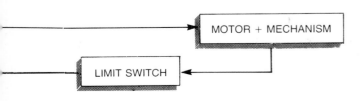

SYSTEMS

Designing as a system

The **aim of designing** is: to attempt to satisfy a human need; to solve a problem; to make a device to do a job to the satisfaction of the user. You should be aware that technology cannot solve all human problems. Often, technological solutions cause other problems. Many problems are to do with relationships between people and countries and need a generous offering of love and understanding!

Solutions to problems come from a **thinking process** which involves making use of known information, finding new information and making new links between the two.

In systems terms it looks like this:

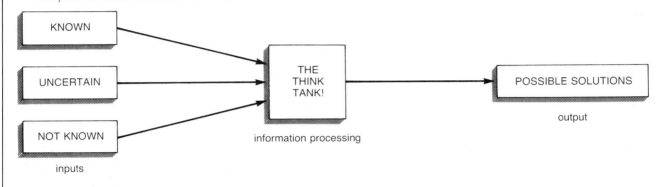

Generating alternative solutions

The **think tank** often needs some help in finding new solutions. Here are four methods you can try.

1 Brainstorming

This is best done in a group. Each person throws an idea or a thought into the 'pool' without any judgement or criticism being made. Any idea is acceptable. Even apparently silly ideas may be useful in stimulating ideas for real possibilities.

2 Family tree

This is similar to brainstorming but can be done on your own. The problem is named and written in the centre of a large sheet of paper. Any connecting idea or area of interest is written down around the problem, and further connections found.

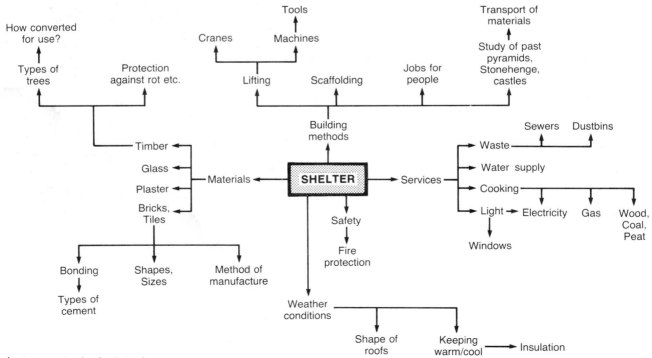

▲ *An example of a 'family tree'*

3 Random word match

A word (noun) is found at random from a book (a non-technological book is better). A connection is then found between the word and the problem being solved. The connections found can be considered as possible solutions or parts of solutions.

The random word: 'flute'
The problem: Greenhouse temperature control (as on page 10).
Possible connections: The controller sounds a warning note at very low temperatures if the heater is not coping: the greenhouse could be heated by hot air through a pipe.

4 What if?

A silly proposal is made, then its good and bad points are looked at without any decision being made as to whether the proposal can be used or not. Good points must be found first! All the points raised help to break out of 'thought blocks'.

A silly proposal: 'All houses should be built with exactly the same shape, plan and materials.'
Good points: Low architects' fees; no problems with planning permission; all components readily available; builders will be experienced; people won't have to visit to inspect layout.
Bad points: Towns would be visually boring; number of rooms would not suit all sizes of families; no scope for architects' imagination.

▲ *Discussion group*

▲ *Not what it seems! An optical illusion in the Science Museum*

Activities

1 Find the connections. **Problem**: Retrieval of small parts from difficult positions. **Random word**: 'drawbridge'.

2 Write down the good and bad points about this proposal: 'Purchases from shops must be made with electronic cards only'.

SYSTEMS

Design factors

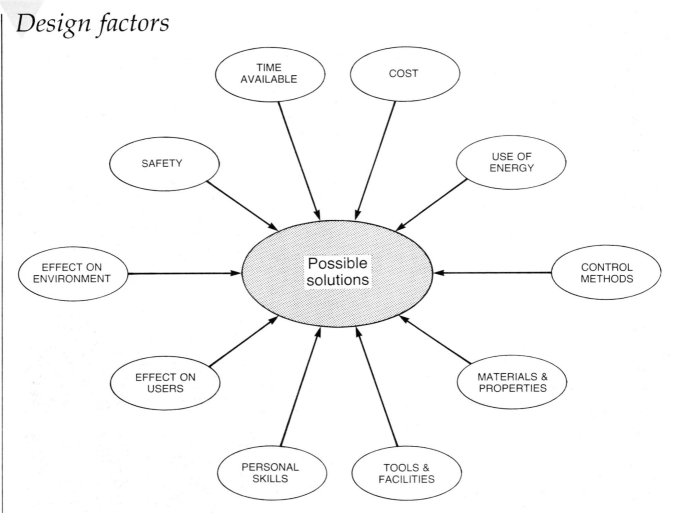

Once a number of possible solutions have been proposed, they need to be looked at in more detail. Some of the factors which need to be considered are shown above. One method of comparing the suitability of solutions is to use a **factor matrix**. The most important factors are written down. Each possible solution is given a score for each factor (1 = very poor, up to 5 = very good). The total score for each solution gives some indication of relative suitability.

Proposed Solution	Factors considered						Total score
	Durable?	Inside and outside use?	Clear display?	Cost of making	Ease of making	Portable?	
PRESSURE TRANSDUCER	4	3	3	2	3	1	16
STRAIN GAUGE	2	4	4	4	2	3	19
CONDUCTIVE FOAM	4	2	3	3	4	2	18

Problem: to measure forces on athletes' legs (see photograph on page 47)

▲ An example of a factor matrix table

Test yourself on . . . . systems

1 Draw a block diagram and identify the **input**, **process** and **output** in the following items.
   a a cooking timer
   b a vacuum cleaner
   c a corn-grinding watermill
   d a motor car
   e an intruder alarm
   f a theatre

2 Identify one or more **subsystems** in the above process blocks.

3 Design the following systems using block diagrams.
   a A child's toy which squeaks once when a light is shone at it.
   b A greenhouse environment which has a ventilation fan to prevent overheating and automatic blinds to prevent the plants from being scorched in the sun.
   c An automatic garage door for a disabled driver. The door should open when the car passes through an infra-red beam.

You will probably find yourself thinking of ways of improving these systems! Remember there is no such thing as a perfect system. There is no need, at this stage, to understand the complete workings of the system. Research will be necessary later to find practical ways of achieving your designs.

4 Make a list of the important things that need to be considered when designing each of the following items.
   a a toy for children under 5 years old
   b a processed and packaged food product
   c a navigation aid for dinghy sailors
   d a board game for families

(See pages 48, 50 and 51, for Appropriate technology *and* Crossing a river.)

ENERGY

Energy does a job of work! If something moves it needs an energy input to start it off. If an object gains in temperature, there must be an energy input to it.

Energy cannot be seen or touched but its effects can be observed or measured. Energy exists in many different forms and can be changed from one form to another.

All processes which use energy produce some waste, but energy cannot be destroyed; it usually ends up as low-level heat which is of no practical use.

Cooling towers at a power station ▼

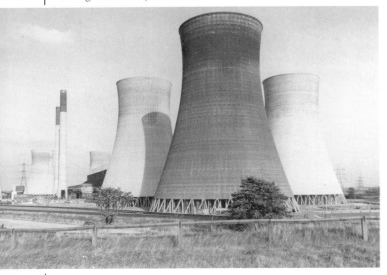

Sources and choices

The most important sources of energy are:
- direct solar   • fossil and nuclear fuels
- moving fluids (water and air).

All energy owes its origin to the Sun. The direct light and heat from the Sun are obvious sources. Coal, one of the fossil fuels, came from decayed plant life which originally grew because of the photosynthesis due to the Sun. Without evaporation from the oceans followed by rain we would have no rivers. The pattern of our weather derives from the Sun.

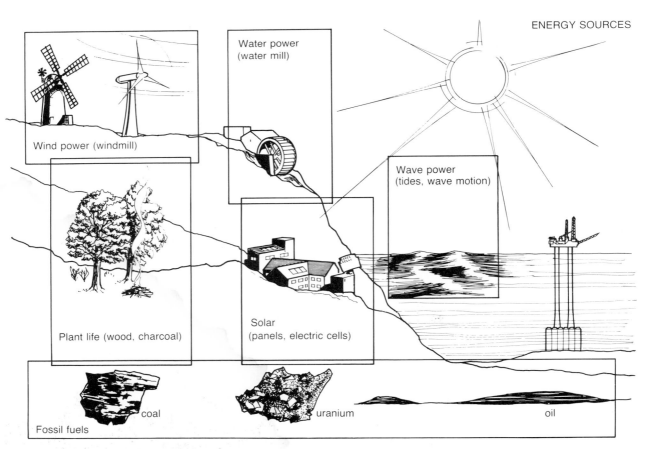

ENERGY SOURCES

Wind power (windmill)

Water power (water mill)

Wave power (tides, wave motion)

Plant life (wood, charcoal)

Solar (panels, electric cells)

Fossil fuels — coal — uranium — oil

▲ *Energy Sources*

Energy in the UK

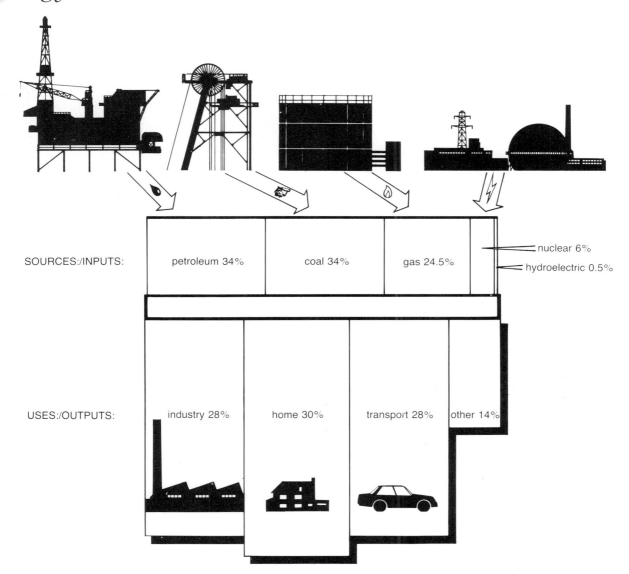

SOURCES:/INPUTS: petroleum 34%   coal 34%   gas 24.5%   nuclear 6%   hydroelectric 0.5%

USES:/OUTPUTS: industry 28%   home 30%   transport 28%   other 14%

▲ *Sources and uses of energy from fuels in the UK*   (Source: 'Digest of UK Energy Statistics' 1986)

Activity

Using electricity and gas bills, find out how much **energy** is being used in your home every day. What difference is there between the summer and winter energy use?

Energy converting systems

Fuels are of little use as energy sources unless they are converted into a useful form, such as heat. A large number of technological devices are **energy converters**.

Original form of energy	Device/process	Converted form of energy*
Light	Plants (photosynthesis)	Chemical
Chemical	Battery	Electrical
Chemical	Heat engine	Mechanical (kinetic)
Electrical	Lamp	Light
Chemical	Power station	Electricity
Potential	Hydropower station	Electricity
Electrical	Loudspeaker	Sound

* This is the main or useful form of energy from the conversion

Waste it, lose it

There are always unwanted **by-products** in energy conversions. For example, in a power station, high pressure steam is produced to drive turbines in order to generate electricity. When the steam has been used it is at a lower temperature and pressure. Its heat is wasted by warming up the atmosphere, although in some places some of the heat is used for community heating. It is not possible to use all of the energy.

Did you know?

The first steam-driven power station was set up by Thomas Edison, in New York, in 1881.

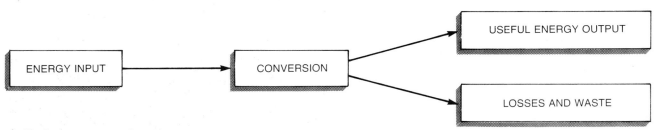

▲ *Practical energy conversion system*

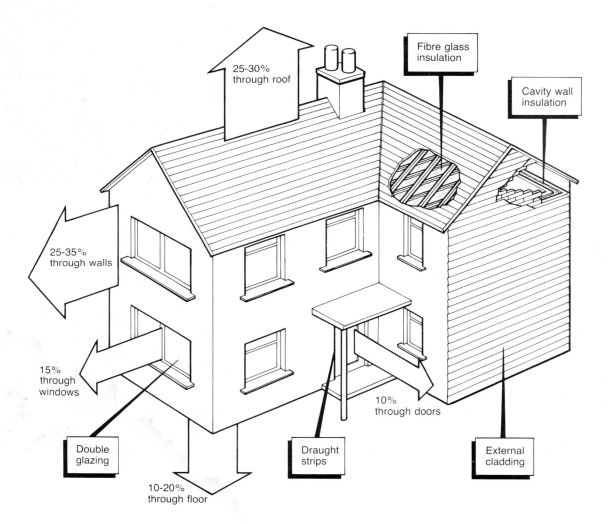

▲ *Heat losses and energy savers in the home*

Save it, use it

Because most of our present-day consumption of energy involves fossil fuels, it is important to use energy-saving techniques in designing. Much of our energy is lost as heat from poorly insulated homes and factories.

Efficiency

To get some idea of how good a device is at converting energy, the concept of **efficiency** is used. Knowing that energy cannot be destroyed, the information in the practical energy conversion system diagram on page 20 can be written as an equation:

ENERGY IN = ENERGY OUT + LOSSES

The greater the losses, the less efficient the conversion. The fraction of ENERGY OUT can be written as a percentage of the ENERGY IN:

$$\text{EFFICIENCY} = \frac{\text{ENERGY OUT}}{\text{ENERGY IN}} \times 100\%$$

For example, a petrol engine in a modern car has an efficiency of about 25%. This means that 75% of the energy input from the fuel is lost; much of it in the form of heat through the radiator. In the winter some of this is used to heat the inside of the car.

Alternatives

There are some problems in the future of fossil fuels, particularly oil and gas. Some estimates give oil from 50 to 100 years before supplies become short, even allowing for new discoveries. Increasingly, technologists are looking for **replacement sources**. This area is a rich resource for school projects as much of the information is readily available.

Nuclear power

Nuclear power is a recent alternative source of energy. It has the great advantage of needing very little fuel, and some processes make the fuel for other nuclear power stations. There are very real problems about making sure that the stations are safe and in the disposal of radioactive waste.

▲ *Solar collectors at the Alternative Technology Centre*

▲ *A nuclear power station*

▲ *Solar battery charger*

Solar power

Even in our northern climates there is appreciable energy from the Sun (during daylight hours!). It has been estimated that sufficient energy falls on the whole surface of an average house roof to provide for half the hot water needs for a family. Practically, not all the direct solar power (some 100 watts per square metre on average) can be utilised. It would be ideal if some way could be found of storing the excess heat of summer, to make up for the colder days in winter.

Some devices are illustrated, which make use of the direct energy from the Sun to heat water, melt metals and produce electricity.

ENERGY

(See also colour page 49 for Tide and wave power.)

Activity

Make a simple solar collector from a black plastic bag filled with a known quantity of water. Put it in direct sunlight and measure the rise in temperature of the water after one hour.

Calculate the amount of energy absorbed per hour.

Energy = mass × specific heat × rise in temperature

Wind power

Windmills have been in use for thousands of years. The simplest type has between four and eight sails made of canvas fastened to the spokes of a wooden wheel. With the addition of modern elastic ropes and the natural tendency of canvas to flap in strong winds, even an apparently crude machine has very efficient safety devices.

With suitable locations, modern large propeller type wind machines have developed up to 3 megawatts. The main problem is the variation of wind speed.

Domestic windmills are used to generate electricity to charge batteries or to heat water. There are experiments to produce heat directly by the friction of paddles in water.

Did you know?

The average family in Britain uses about 10 000 million joules of energy to heat water every year.

▲ *Some different types of wind generator*

▲ *The power of the wind*

▲ *The 130 kW vertical axis wind-turbine at Carmarthen Bay*

Water power

Falling water has been used to drive wheels for over two thousand years. The Romans developed simple 'peg and lantern' gearing which allowed the wheel to be supported horizontally. Even small, slow-moving streams had their corn and gunpowder grinding mills in the 16th century. One of the author's local rivers, the Wandle, had about 90 mills in its six mile length in 1831, although the remains of only four mills exist today!

Many developments and experiments have led to the modern high speed turbine used in hydroelectric power schemes.

Activities

1 Find out if there are any water mills near to your home. How do they work? How is the water directed to the wheel?

2 Make a model waterwheel and investigate the power output by generating electricity (see page 45, Measurement)

▲ Electricity from water power at Rudyard Kipling's house, Batemans, Kent. Water flows through the turbine at 15 litres per second to generate 1500 watts.

Plants

Energy from the Sun is stored in plant material by the process of photosynthesis. This process is used to produce food (human fuel!) and wood for burning. Plant sugars can be distilled to make alcohol (ethanol) as a vehicle fuel. The remains of plants can be composted. A mixture of plant remains and animal manure can be rotted at 36°C in a closed container by the action of bacteria. Methane gas is released which can be burnt or used as an engine fuel.

Did you know?

1 kilogram of poultry manure can produce 1.2 cubic metres of methane!

Rubbish

Western societies produce a large amount of rubbish. Some is **recycled**, but much of it is burnt. The energy produced from such burning could provide heating for homes, greenhouses etc. In fact, burning is the only way to dispose of many plastics materials which do not decompose. A number of carefully controlled refuse units are in operation and some also recover useful metals for reprocessing.

▲ Fuel pellets made from household and industrial rubbish

Geothermal

Underneath the earth's crust there is an extremely hot molten layer. Since the earth's formation it has been cooling down very slowly. At weak spots in the crust, evidence of this heat is seen in volcanic activity. In some countries, for example Iceland and New Zealand, use is made of hot springs for domestic heating. It is also possible (but not commercially practical at present) to extract heat from the Earth by drilling down some 3000 metres and circulating water through two adjacent bore holes.

Hot steam for free! A geyser in new Zealand ▶

Practical power for projects

Many school projects need a source of energy for movement, etc. Here are a few suggestions.

Potential energy can be **stored** in:
- a raised weight (solid or liquid)
- a wound coil spring (e.g. clockwork)
- a stretched elastic band or membrane (e.g. a balloon)
- compressed air.

Electrical energy can be **converted** by:
- an electrical motor (rotary motion)
- a solenoid (linear motion).

Electrical energy can be **stored** in:
- dry cells (batteries)
- rechargeable cells
- capacitors.

(*Note* Accumulators, e.g. car batteries, are not recommended for school projects because of their acid contents and high current outputs.)

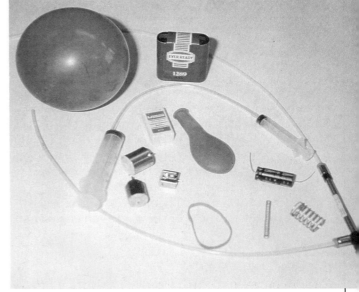

▲ *Some energy sources for projects*

Test yourself on . . . . energy

1 Find out the amount of fuel used in your home or school every year, and the cost per megajoule.
2 Find out the costs of each of the energy saving methods shown on page 20. Can you say which methods are **cost effective**? Which of them need expert installation?

3 What form of alternative energy might be suitable for the following locations?
   a the Sahara desert
   b the Scottish Highlands
   c the centre of a large city
   d a swimming pool on a camping site

```
INPUT SETTING  →  CONTROL PROCESS  →  CONTROL DEVICE
```

Open loop control

Loops and feedback

There are a large number of devices in everyday life which have to be controlled. Lights need to be switched on and off. The water flow from a tap needs to be controlled. When cooking, the heat from a gas flame needs to be adjusted. The typewriter is a controlled mechanism.

Most of the devices controlled by people come in a group known as **open loop control**. The input is set, the process happens and the output that follows cannot always be exactly predicted. It may or may not be suitable, and can only be checked with the human senses. If you turn a tap on and get soaked unexpectedly, you have been a victim of an open loop and have to rely on quick muscular reactions! In order to improve our control of the environment we need to measure the actual **output response** and compare it with the **intended response**. We do this naturally when we learn to walk and later to ride a bike or drive a car. Our senses 'feed back' the response to the brain which 'computes' the necessary adjustments to the muscles.

ONE OF THESE TAPS MUST HAVE AN OPEN LOOP!!!

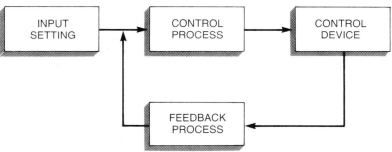

▲ *Feedback added*

The use of **feedback** in a system defines **closed loop control** and is the basis for automatic control. A measurement is made of the output and this is compared with the desired output. The input to the process is then automatically adjusted to make the output correct.

There are problems about feedback. Ideally the adjustment due to feedback should happen instantly, but in real systems it usually takes some time. The adjustment **lags** behind the change in output. Wild changes in output because of changes in loading on a motor, for example, can be over-adjusted. If the feedback increases the output when it should be decreasing it, the system becomes **unstable**. The 'howl' from an audio amplifier system is a good example of this.

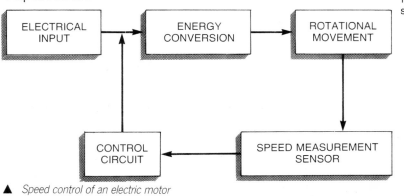

▲ *Speed control of an electric motor*

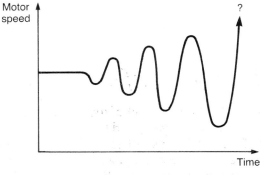

▲ *Unstable speed control of a motor caused by increasing positive feedback*

Control processes

Stop/Go

Electrical

There are a large number of electrical switches with different mechanical arrangements, but all connect or disconnect the power in a circuit. **Changeover** (double throw) **switches** are particularly useful for controlling two devices (see Logic 'OR' page 34). **Rotary switches** are available to control up to 12 devices.

Some electrical switches ▶

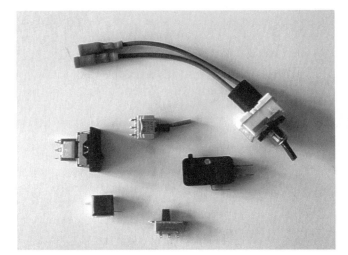

Mechanical

The action of the **clutch** is to disconnect motion from a drive shaft. This is just one example of mechanical control.

Lawnmower clutches ▶

Pneumatic

Both two and three-port **valves** will switch compressed air to a cylinder. The three-port valve is used with double acting cylinders where exhaust air travels in the reverse direction through the pipe.

Two and three-port valves ▶

Speed restriction

Electrical

The flow of electric current in a circuit is controlled by the total resistance in the circuit. A **variable resistor** is useful for controlling the brightness of lamps and for the simple speed control of motors (the control at low speeds is poor with this method and can be improved by **pulsing** the input i.e. switching it on and off rapidly).

▲ *Variable resistors*

Mechanical

The speed of a mechanical device can be controlled by **brakes** i.e. by changing the **frictional force** applied to a drum or disc attached to a shaft.

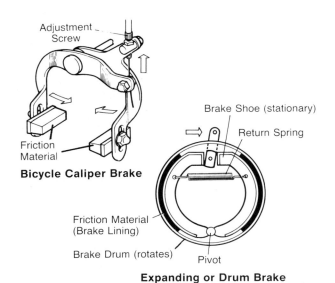

Bicycle Caliper Brake

Expanding or Drum Brake

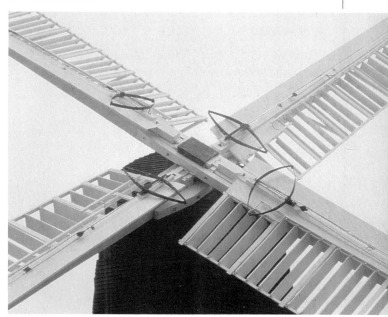

▲ *The speed control on this windmill opens the shutters when the wind pressure increases*

Pneumatic

Throttles or **restrictors** vary the quantity of air supplied to the cylinder, to slow the speed of the piston.

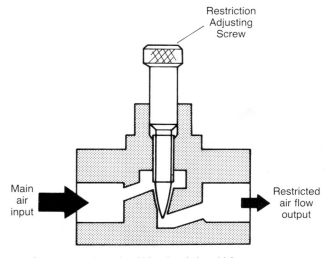

▲ *Cross-section through a bidirectional air restrictor*

Activity

Design a system to test the effectiveness of bicycle brakes. One factor you will need to take into account is the speed of the wheels before braking. What other factors might affect the braking?

CONTROL

One way

Electrical

At low voltages the **diode** can be regarded as a device which allows current only in one direction. A light emitting diode (LED) has the same action, but at a much lower voltage.

(**Note**: For a 1N4001 Silicon type: less than 50 volts and a maximum of 1 amp. For a standard 5 mm LED: maximum reverse voltage is 5 volts and maximum current 30 milliamps.)

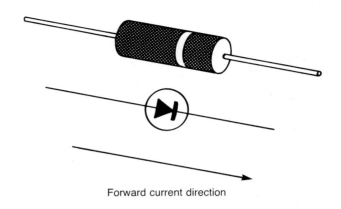

Forward current direction

▲ *A typical silicon diode*

Mechanical

A **ratchet** limits rotary motion to one direction. A **worm and worm-wheel** arrangement ensures that the drive is only from the worm to the worm-wheel.

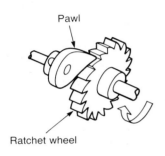

Pawl

Ratchet wheel

▲ *Ratchet*

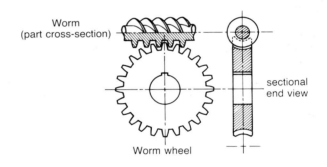

Worm (part cross-section)

sectional end view

Worm wheel

▲ *Worm drive*

Pneumatic

The non-return valve contains a ball which allows air through in one direction but blocks it in the other. These are often combined with restrictors, to give restriction in one direction and free flow in the other.

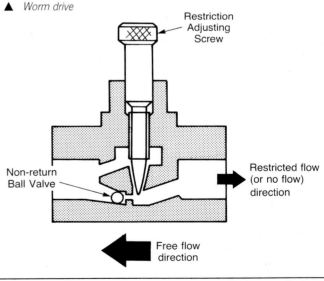

Restriction Adjusting Screw

Non-return Ball Valve

Restricted flow (or no flow) direction

Free flow direction

Unidirectional restrictor ▶

Activity

Connect two different coloured LEDs in parallel as in the diagram. Reverse the 1½ volt cell. What did you observe?

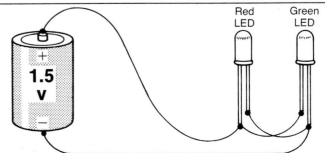

Red LED

Green LED

1.5 V

Delays

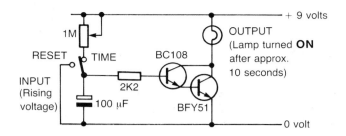

OUTPUT
(Lamp turned **ON**
after approx.
10 seconds)

1M

RESET   TIME   BC108

INPUT
(Rising
voltage)   2K2   BFY51

100 µF

+ 9 volts

0 volt

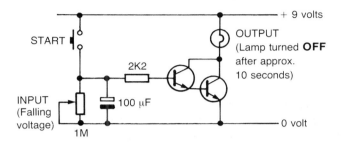

+ 9 volts

START

2K2   OUTPUT
(Lamp turned **OFF**
after approx.
10 seconds)

INPUT
(Falling
voltage)   100 µF

1M   0 volt

Electrical

The **capacitor** is the component in a circuit which is
used to obtain a time delay, from microseconds to
hours, as it needs time to store electrical energy. The
larger the value (in farads) of capacitance the longer
the value of time delay. Typical circuits are shown in
the diagram.

Electronic time delay circuits ▶

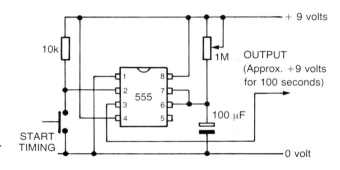

+ 9 volts

10k

1M   OUTPUT
(Approx. +9 volts
for 100 seconds)

555

100 µF

START
TIMING   0 volt

Mechanical

There are a number of devices which will slow or
damp motion. The most well known is the pendulum
driven escapement in clocks. A **dashpot** is useful for
controlling linear motion by the gradual leakage of
air or oil from a small hole in a piston.

A simple dashpot ▶

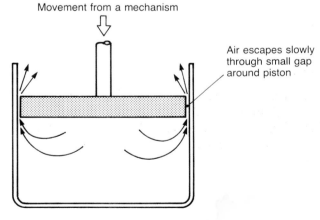

Movement from a mechanism

Air escapes slowly
through small gap
around piston

Pneumatic

The **reservoir** (a strong metal 'can' with connections
at each end) in a pneumatic circuit acts in a similar
way to the capacitor. The air pressure gradually
builds up until it is sufficient to operate a
pressure-sensitive valve.

Pneumatic time delay ▶

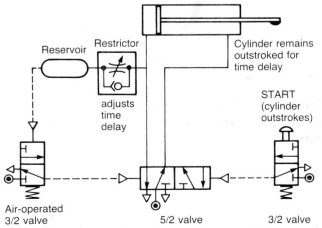

Reservoir   Restrictor   Cylinder remains
outstroked for
time delay

adjusts
time
delay

START
(cylinder
outstrokes)

Air-operated
3/2 valve   5/2 valve   3/2 valve

CONTROL

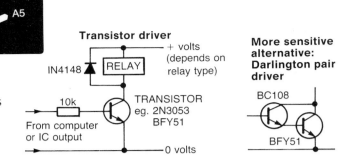

Interchange

It is often useful to control one type of device with another. For example to control rotary motion by an electronic input. To do this an intermediate device is necessary, often called an **interface**.

Electronic to Electrical

Integrated circuits and **computer outputs** work at low currents (typically, 1 mA and less) and can be interfaced with higher current devices by the arrangements shown in the diagram.

Transistor driver

IN4148 RELAY + volts (depends on relay type)

10k TRANSISTOR eg. 2N3053 BFY51

From computer or IC output

0 volts

More sensitive alternative: Darlington pair driver

BC108

BFY51

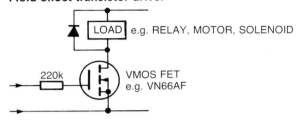

Field effect transistor driver

LOAD e.g. RELAY, MOTOR, SOLENOID

220k VMOS FET e.g. VN66AF

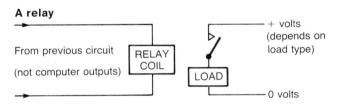

A relay

From previous circuit (not computer outputs)

RELAY COIL

LOAD

+ volts (depends on load type)

0 volts

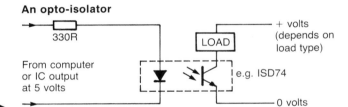

An opto-isolator

330R

From computer or IC output at 5 volts

LOAD e.g. ISD74

+ volts (depends on load type)

0 volts

Interface devices ▶

Electrical to Mechanical and Pneumatic

Solenoids are electromagnets with movable centres or end levers. A typical 12 volt solenoid could provide a 12 to 18 mm linear movement with a force of 3 newtons. A **solenoid valve** uses the movement to open and close a valve to control pneumatics or hydraulics.

Solenoids ▶

Mechanical and Pneumatic to Electrical

The motion of devices can trigger **microswitches** or magnetically operated **reed switches** to control such as indicator lights and the extent of movement.

Microswitch and reed switch ▶

Mechanical to Mechanical

A number of methods of converting rotary to linear motion and linear to rotary motion are shown in the diagram.

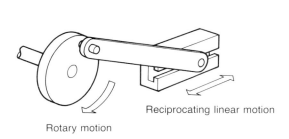

Reciprocating linear motion

Rotary motion

▲ *Crank and slider*

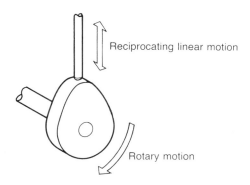

Reciprocating linear motion

Rotary motion

▲ *Disc cam and follower*

Rotary motion

Linear motion

▲ *Rack and pinion*

Safety

All devices should be designed to **fail** in a **safe** condition. Here are some of the methods of achieving this.

Electrical

A **fuse** is placed in the live supply wire to a device to protect the supply cable from excess current if the device fails or short circuits. The rating printed on a fuse is the safe, normal working current. Miniature **circuit breakers** are used as alternatives to fuses.

◀ *Circuit breaker*

Mechanical

Pulley systems are often used in situations where damage may occur to a mechanism if the driven device stops dead. If the chuck of a drilling machine or a lathe is jammed the motor will not be stalled if the belt drive is able to slip.

Another mechanical safety device is the **shear pin**. A small pin is used to connect a gear to the driven shaft. The pin will break if there is excess **torque** (turning force).

Drilling machine drive pulleys ▶

Pneumatic

A **safety valve** is used in fluid systems to release excess pressure.

A safety valve on a compressor ▶

Logic

Some processes need to respond to more than one input at one time. **Logic** is a useful way of dealing with a combination of different inputs. It can be applied to electrical switches, pneumatic valves or electronics. There are three basic logic functions: **AND**, **OR** and **NOT**. Other functions can be made by combination. The required **logic function** can be found simply by describing the process in words, and looking for **AND, OR** and **NOT**. Logic functions are also referred to as **gates**.

AND logic

*The garage door will open only if the car breaks a light beam **and** the horn sounds.* This requirement identifies two inputs with an **AND** logic function.

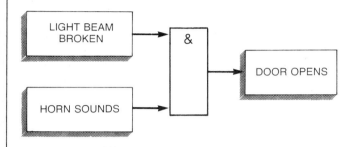

Electrical switches

In the circuit shown in the diagram, both switch A **AND** switch B must be closed to light the bulb that is to give an output.

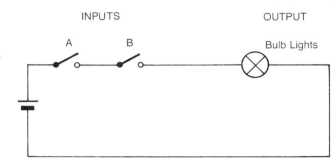

Pneumatic valves

A safety system is required for example for a press machine. The operators must push both valves together so that their hands are not trapped by the machine.

Both valve A **AND** valve B must be kept pressed to operate the cylinder.

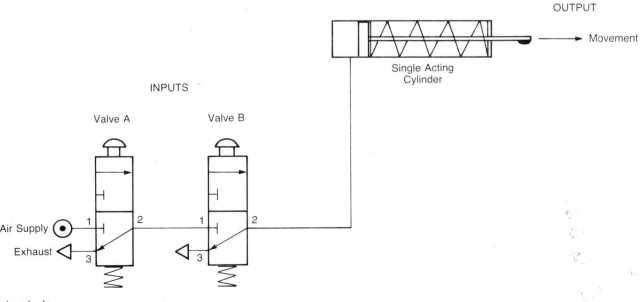

Activity

Find some more examples of systems where two or more inputs must occur at the same time for the system to work. Write a description of each system in the form: 'Both . . . **AND** . . . must happen in order to . . .'.

CONTROL

AND logic

Electronics

One of the digital **integrated circuits** (ICs) which uses the **AND** function is the 7408. This contains four **AND** gates, each with two inputs. Integrated circuits can be obtained with three inputs or more.

With the 7408 and other similar ICs an 'input' (logic '1') is usually at 5 volts and 'no input' (logic '0') is at 0 volts. If both inputs are connected to 5 volts then there will be an output. If either or both inputs are connected to 0 volts there will be no output.

(See data page 86 for outline diagrams of common integrated circuits.)

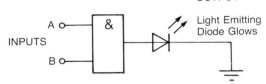

Schematic diagram

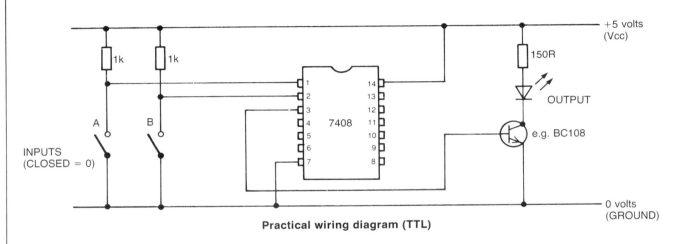

Practical wiring diagram (TTL)

OR logic

Electrical switches

'A person wants a buzzer to sound if a caller arrives at **either** the front **or** back door of a house', identifies two inputs with an **OR** logic function.

In the circuit shown in the diagram, either switch A **OR** switch B can be closed to sound the buzzer.
An alternative way of making an **OR** function with a relay is shown in the second diagram.

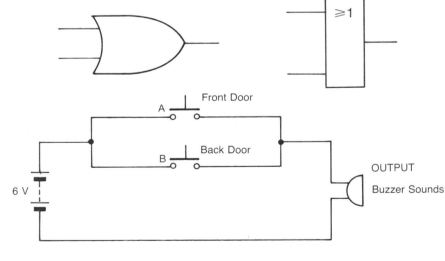

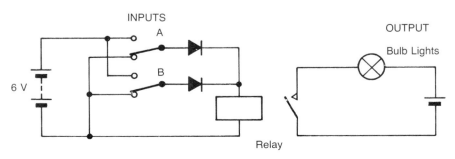

Pneumatic valves

A door is required to be opened from either one side or the other.

In the circuit shown in the diagram, either valve A **OR** valve B can be pressed to operate the cylinder and open the door. The **shuttle valve** is necessary to prevent air from one valve exhausting through the other valve.

Underground train's door opening button ▶

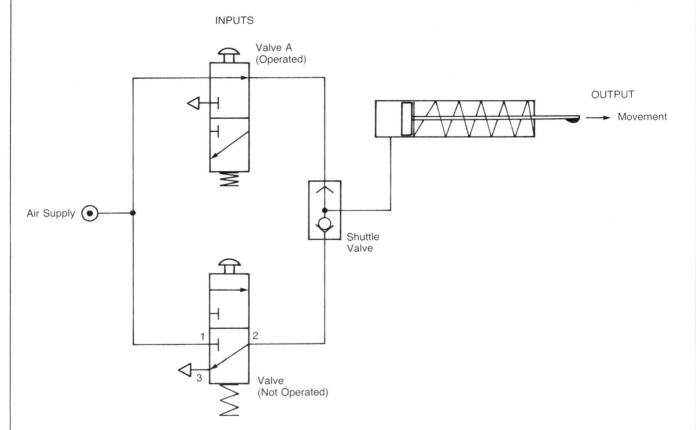

Electronics

The 7432 IC contains four two-input **OR** gates. In each gate, if either input is connected to 5 volts there will be an output.

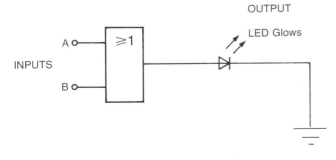

Schematic diagram

CONTROL

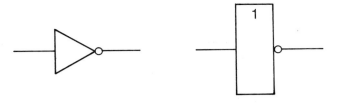

NOT logic

When a refrigerator door is closed, the internal lamp must **NOT** be alight. When a door or window is in place, the intruder alarm must **NOT** sound.

Logical **NOT** is also known as an **inverter**. When there is an input there will be no output. When there is no input, there will be an output.

Electrical

In the circuit shown in the diagram, when the switch is closed the bulb will **NOT** be alight. (Resistor R is to limit the current flow through the bulb and so prevent a short circuit when the switch is closed.)

Switches or valves can be obtained which switch off when pressed. In **relays** and other electrical switches, the contacts will be labelled 'normally closed'.

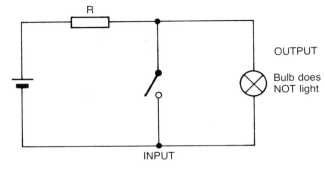

Switch ON

Electronics

The 7404 IC contains six inverters. In each inverter if the input is connected to 5 volts there will be no output.

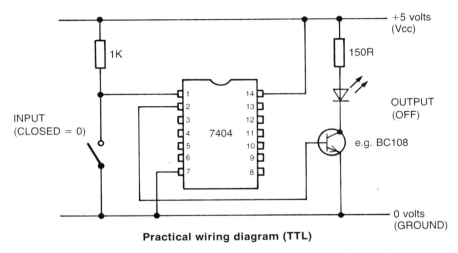

Practical wiring diagram (TTL)

Pneumatics

Special air operated **NOT** valves are available or a 5-port pilot-operated valve can be used as shown in the diagram.

NOT Valve

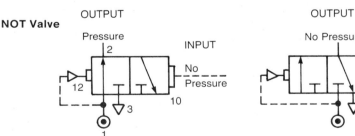

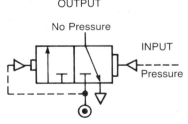

5/2 way Pilot Air-Operated Valve

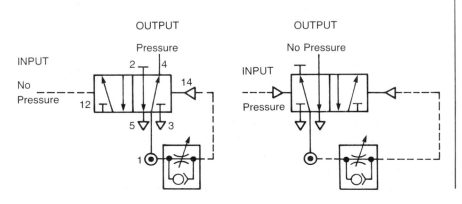

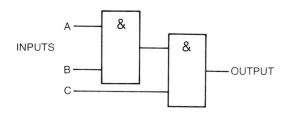

A three-input AND gate using two two-input gates

A	B	C	OUTPUT
0	0	0	0
0	0	1	0
0	1	0	0
0	1	1	0
1	0	0	0
1	0	1	0
1	1	0	0
1	1	1	1

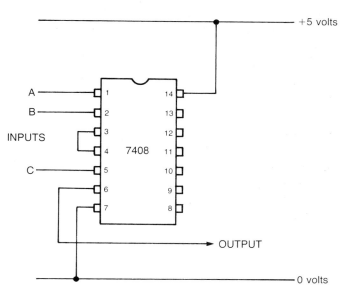

Practical wiring diagram (TTL)

Combining logic inputs

All logic gates have two or more inputs except **NOT** gates or inverters which always have one input. If only two input gates are available, more inputs can be obtained by combining gates. In fact, when using **digital integrated circuits** this is an advantage, as one IC will usually contain more than one gate, and extra power connections are not required.

The three basic logic functions, **AND**, **OR** and **NOT**, can be combined to give a required response to several different inputs. This is where things can get madly complicated, but using **truth tables** usually helps to sort out the output. A truth table shows the output from a logic gate for a given set of inputs.

The diagram illustrates this requirement: *When the sun is shining and it is not raining, indicate that the washing may be hung out to dry.*

Sunshine = logic 1   Rain sensed = logic 1

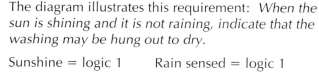

Activity

Work out another logic system to include the wind *not* blowing the washing off the clothes-line! Then think about the possibility of an alarm to indicate that the washing should be brought in.

CONTROL

Further electronic logic

It is sometimes convenient to use only one type of logic IC and to combine the gates to form all the others required. One of the easiest gates to manufacture is the **NAND**, which is an **AND** gate followed by a **NOT** (e.g. 7400 or 4011 ICs).

The table shows the combinations and truth tables of all the other logic functions and how **NAND** gates can be combined.

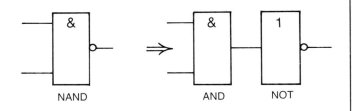

▲ Using NAND

Logic Function	Logic Symbol	B.S. Symbol	Truth Table			Circuit using NAND Gates only
			INPUTS		OUTPUT	
			B	A	Y	
AND			0	0	0	
			0	1	0	
			1	0	0	
			1	1	1	
OR			0	0	0	
			0	1	1	
			1	0	1	
			1	1	1	
NOT				0	1	
				1	0	
NAND			0	0	1	
			0	1	1	
			1	0	1	
			1	1	0	
NOR			0	0	1	
			0	1	0	
			1	0	0	
			1	1	0	
XOR			0	0	0	
			0	1	1	
			1	0	1	
			1	1	0	
XNOR			0	0	1	
			0	1	0	
			1	0	0	
			1	1	1	

38

Programmed control

A **programme** is a logical sequence of instructions. Many control situations can be achieved without programming. For example a floor **turtle** or buggy designed to follow a white line can be controlled by two light sensors and circuitry driving **steering motors**. If the buggy was to be designed to do other tasks in the future, in other words, to be **versatile**, it may be an advantage to drive it with a **programmable device**.

Child's 'record-player' musical box with programmed disc ▶

Programmes can be altered to suit changed circumstances: perhaps to give different time delays, or to sense different conditions.

An example of a simple programmable device is a musical box, where a series of pins hit the notes in the right sequence to produce a tune.

A cam-operated piece of fun! Made by Paul Spooner ▶

CONTROL

Computer control

Industry is making use of new technology by developing computer-controlled assembly lines and also heavy duty precision **robots** to do repetitive jobs. Robots are often used in difficult or dangerous environments.

Most **personal computers**, with **user** (add-on) **ports**, can send and receive signals to the outside world. The user port is normally a **memory-mapped** device. This means that information can be placed in a particular **location** in the memory for output, or the location can be inspected for input.

The **BBC computer** will be used as the example for the remainder of this section. It is an '8 bit' machine, that is the memory locations contain eight **binary digits**. Each bit has a **decimal equivalent weighting**, so that all the numbers between 0 and 255 can be stored. The bits are usually numbered 0 to 7 because the weighting is equal to 2 raised to the power of the bit number. For example, bit 2 is weighted 2^2 which equals 4.

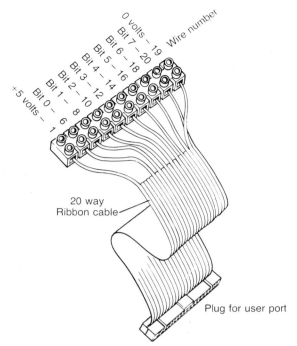

▲ User port connections and terminal block

▼ 8 bits and decimal equivalents

Bit number	7	6	5	4	3	2	1	0
Decimal	128	64	32	16	8	4	2	1

Pin/Wire	2	3	5	7	9	11	13	15	17
Connection	0 V	Bit 0	Bit 1	Bit 2	Bit 3	Bit 4	Bit 5	Bit 6	Bit 7

▲ Printer port connections (for output only)

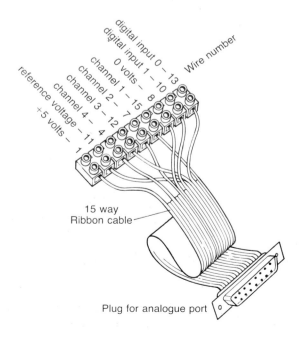

▲ Analogue port digital connections

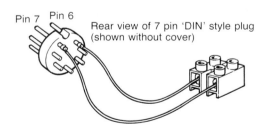

▲ Cassette socket connection

The location of the user port in the BBC model B and Master Series computers is at the address **65120** (if you are used to **hexadecimal numbers**, 65120 = **&FE60**.

For connections to the user port, you will need, for experimental use, a 20-way 'bump polarised' socket (RS components No. 474-300) and some 20-way ribbon cable for connection to a 2 amp terminal block.

Input to the user port

Any simple switch can be connected to the computer, provided that you are careful to use the correct wires into the user port.

Activity

Attach a single-pole switch of any type to Bit 0 of the user port of a computer as in diagram. Use **PRINT ?65120** to see the result of switching 'on'.

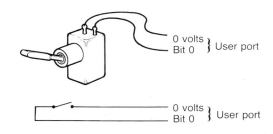

Output from the user port

The current output from the computer is not sufficient to drive most devices, so an interface is needed (see also page 30). A single transistor interface is useful for experimentation with one bit output, but for **multiple bit control** a Darlington Driver (ULN2803) IC is better.

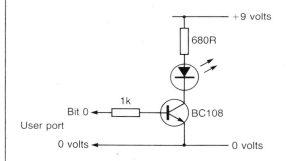

▲ *Single transistor interface*

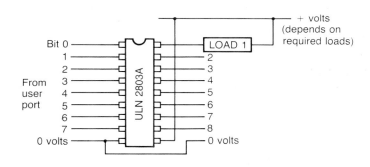

▲ *Darlington Driver IC interface*

The user port IC has to be informed that outputs are needed, by placing a number in address **65122** (**&FE62**). The number corresponds to the total decimal weighting of the bits required for output.

?65122 = 255 labels all bits as outputs

?65122 = 15   labels bits 0,1,2 and 3 as outputs only (15 is obtained from 1 + 2 + 4 + 8)

?65120 = 8   switches bit 3 'on' as output

Activity

a Connect an LED to the user port using a transistor interface and switch it on and off from a simple program.

b Combine an input switch with an LED output, so that the LED goes on 10 seconds after the switch has been closed.

CONTROL

For more complicated computer control it is better to use a commercial interface which has protection on inputs and outputs.

When using relays with transistor interfaces, a diode must be in place to protect the transistor from reverse emf. When using motors, a 0.1 μF capacitor across the terminals avoids **interference**.

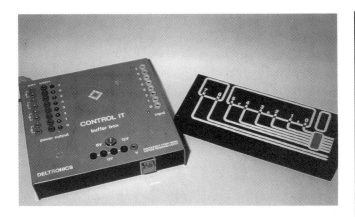

▲ CONTROL-IT and LEGO interfaces

Programming

After direct inputting and outputting, the next step is to be able to build **control programs**. The use of dedicated LOGO-type control programs such as BITS, CONTROL-IT, CONTROL LOGO or LEGO LINES is recommended. These enable the control functions to be understood clearly without needing to understand the BASIC programming language.

Procedures

So that your program can be understood by others, and to avoid muddles, it is advisable to write **structured programs**. This is done by writing a number of short **procedures** which take care of particular parts of the whole control sequence. For example, if you were designing an automatic sorting machine, one procedure could be to recognise the size of the objects; another to operate a mechanism to push an object into a storage bin; another to deal with timing.

Nesting and branching

A set of **nesting procedures** are called up within each other and are useful for **sequential control**. In simple English, nesting can be expressed as: *While procedure A is happening, do procedure B.*

Branching within procedures is done by applying a **condition**. For example, if there is an input on Bit 7, then carry out procedure 'motor'. This would be written in BASIC as:

IF (?65120 AND 128) = 128 THEN PROCmotor ELSE PROClights

If there is no input on Bit 7 then the program branches to the procedure called 'lights'. The purpose of the AND logic is to force the computer to look *only* at Bit 7.

(*Note* Line numbers would, of course, be needed in BASIC for this, and the following examples.)

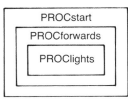

▲ Nested procedures

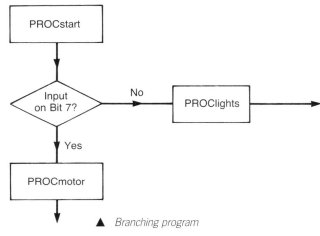

▲ Branching program

Looping

If operations need to be repeated several times, a FOR . . .NEXT **loop** can be used.

```
FOR count=0 TO 10
PROCinput
NEXT count
```

This will repeat the procedure 'input' ten times.

If an operation needs to be continued until a **condition** is met, REPEAT . . .UNTIL (condition) is used.

```
REPEAT
PROCoutput
UNTIL (?65120 AND 128)=128
PROCstop
```

This will continue the procedure 'output' until there is an input on Bit 7, then the procedure 'stop' is executed.

Timing

If your program needs a number of **time delays**, a procedure can be built to deal with this. The procedure is first defined with a variable 'T' in seconds.

```
DEFPROCtime(T)
TIME=0
REPEAT
UNTIL T=TIME/100
ENDPROC
```

The delay procedure is called up within any procedure by giving 'T' a number.

```
?65120=1
PROCtime(6)
?65120=0
```

This will turn 'on' Bit 1, wait 6 seconds then turn Bit 1 'off'.

To find out how long an operation takes, in seconds, first reset the clock with **TIME=0** then insert a line after the operation has finished that will give the **command**, PRINT TIME/100.

Advanced users

The user port only provides eight lines for either input or output or a combination of the two. A further 8 output bits can be obtained by using the printer port (with an interface as before) which is at address **65121 (&FE61)**. An additional single output is obtained by using the **cassette motor drive relay** and the commands ★MOTOR1 to switch on, ★MOTOR0 to switch off.

An additional two digital inputs are to be found at pins X and Y on the analogue port which are checked by **ADVAL(0) AND 3**. This equals 0 for no input, 1 for PB0 input, 2 for PB1 input and 3 for both inputs. Connections are shown in the figures on page 40.

▼ *Computer control of a buggy*

Test yourself on . . . . control

1 Identify whether open or closed loop control is used in the following systems.
   a A bicycle braking system
   b An aquarium heater with a thermostat control
   c The rudder of a sailing dinghy
   d Microcomputer-controlled buggy with revolution counter on axle

2 For each of the systems in **1** which are closed loop, suggest the feedback measurement possible.

3 A student wants a motor to move a lens backwards and forwards in front of a lamp for focusing purposes. Suggest some control devices that might be considered.

4 Select a suitable **logic system** for these situations.
   a The exit barrier from a car park will rise if there is a car waiting to exit and the correct money has been inserted in the coin box.
   b The crossing sequence on a pedestrian crossing must start if the button has been pressed on one side of the road or the other.
   c The central-heating boiler is to switch on if the water in the tank is cool or if the room temperature is low.
   d An automatic watering device in a greenhouse has a pump which will switch on when the soil is dry but not if there is no water in the storage tank.
   e An automatic garage door for a disabled driver should open when the car passes through an infra-red beam and the car horn is sounded.

5 Complete the 'truth' tables for these logic systems:

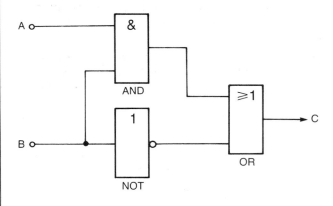

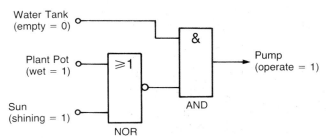

6 Write a programme in BASIC, LOGO or any other control language with which you are familiar, to control these sequences from a computer. (User-port lines are given for each input or output.)

   a Turn on a motor for about 10 seconds. (Motor on Bit 0)

   b Make a light send an SOS signal (· · · — — — · · ·). (Light on Bit 0)

   c Make two lights flash alternately. (Lights on Bits 0 and 1)

   d Turn on a motor 20 seconds after a switch has been closed. (Motor on Bit 0, switch on Bit 7)

   e Turn on a motor and reverse it when a switch is closed. (Motor forward Bit 0 on; motor reversed Bit 0 off and Bit 1 on; switch on Bit 7)

   f A train operates a switch which causes two red lights to flash, then a level crossing barrier (which has a 'barrier closed' switch sensor) is lowered. (Barrier motor on Bit 0; lights on Bits 1 and 1; train sensor on Bit 7; barrier sensor on Bit 6)

▲ *Automatic control of level crossing gates*

Reasons for sense!

Sensors have two functions in systems:
- to act as inputs
- to sense changes in output as part of a feedback loop (see page 25.)

All sensors change an incoming signal to a different form which is easier to use for indication or display. You will find sensors also referred to as **transducers.**

A measurement system looks like this:

▲ *A pupil's test rig for a model water wheel*

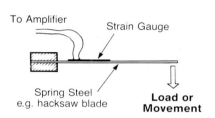

▲ *Calibration of a cantilever using a strain gauge*

How a measurement system should work

Ideally the effect to be measured should be observed without interference to the effect. This is sometimes possible by using **light sensors**, but often the method of measurement 'loads' the system and makes the quantity being measured smaller. An example is shown in the photograph where the pupil is attempting to measure the power output of a model waterwheel. The friction in the bearings and between the gears, and the resistance to motion from the magnets in the motor (being used as a generator), reduce the power output.

Any measurement system needs to be **calibrated**. This means that before an unknown quantity is measured, a known quantity is input and the scale of the meter is marked off with numbers representing the values, or a graph is drawn of the quantity against the displayed reading.

For example, a cantilever with a **strain gauge** for measuring forces can be calibrated by loading with known weights, and the analogue meter marked off in newtons.

Activity

Couple together two small DC motors as in the illustration and measure the input and the output power (equals voltage × current).

What difference do you notice between the two results? What is the reason for the difference?

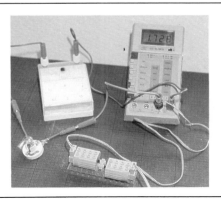

SENSING AND MEASURING

Some common types of measurement transducer

Change from	Change to	Example
Force	Displacement	Spring
Displacement	Electrical resistance	Strain gauge potentiometer
Displacement	Voltage	Generator
Temperature	Electrical resistance	Thermistor
Temperature	Displacement	Mercury thermometer
Temperature	Voltage (emf)	Thermocouple
Light	Electrical resistance	Light dependent resistor
Light	Current	Photodiode
Light	Voltage	Solar cell
Sound	Voltage	Microphone
Pressure	Displacement	Manometer
Pressure or sound	Voltage (emf)	Piezocrystal
Voltage	Angular displacement	Voltmeter

Chaining sensors

The input effect to be measured is not always the most convenient, so a series of changes can be used, and this is known as **chaining**, to give the most suitable unit of measurement.

A cantilever spring can be used to measure forces as the displacement of the end is proportional to the force applied. The displacement can be measured with a **micrometer-type screw**, although this is not particularly sensitive.

The force could be measured more accurately with a strain gauge which changes its resistance with change in length, as the strain in the top surface is proportional to the force applied. In this case, the resistance has to be measured.

Known forces on the cantilever are used to find out how to interpret the resistance for an unknown force.

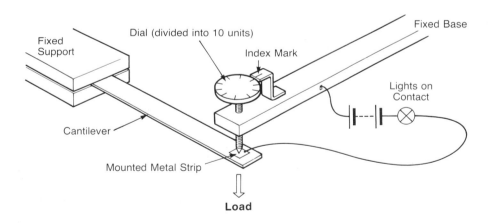

▲ *Calibration of a cantilever using a micrometer-type screw*

Strain gauge applications

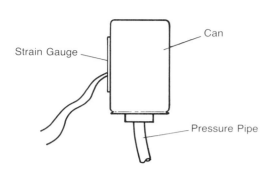

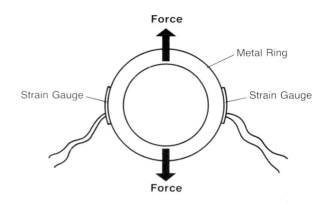

▲ *A proving ring*

In the diagram, the strain gauge is being used to measure the change in size of the can due to the change in pressure. The system is calibrated with a known pressure e.g. heights of water in the tube, or loads on a piston.

The **proving ring** shown has a strain gauge each side for balance and can be used in tensile or compressive testing. Calibration is by using known loads.

Dealing with small signals

The change in resistance in the strain gauge is so small that an electrical meter cannot be used directly. (A meter, of course, changes the signal back into a displacement so that it can be seen!) In this case an **amplifier** has to be used to make the signal larger.

(cont. on page 56)

▼ *Practical strain gauge amplifier*

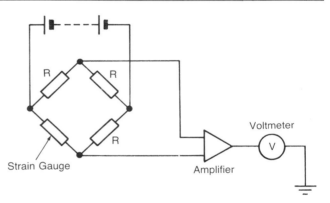

▲ *Schematic of strain gauge amplifier (A small out-of-balance voltage is caused by the change in resistance of the strain gauge)*

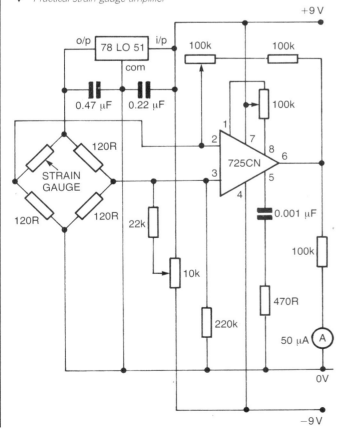

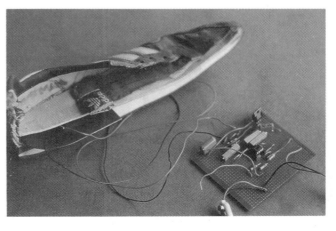

▲ *A strain gauge is used to measure the impact of the heel of the shoe on the ground*

Appropriate technology

The technology must fit the situation and the people for which it is designed. The computer, for example, becomes a very expensive and inappropriate solution if what was really needed was a few switches, or some simple electronics. Also, the **end users** need the knowledge and resources to get the best out of the designed solution. Inappropriate technology is bad design.

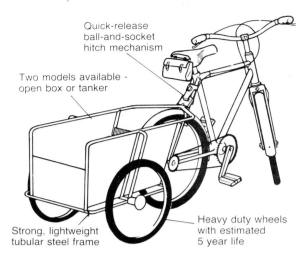

Quick-release
ball-and-socket
hitch mechanism

Two models available -
open box or tanker

Strong, lightweight
tubular steel frame

Heavy duty wheels
with estimated
5 year life

Loaded down?

The photograph shows a bicycle loaded to its limit with pottery. The lack of suitable transport prevents poor people from using their labour productively. Rural people in some countries spend hours of every working day laboriously carrying or pushing loads which could be transported much more efficiently. The obvious solution to this problem might seem to be to use motorised transport, but the purchase price of a car or van would be beyond the earning power of this type of person. The running costs, also, could not be covered by profits from a business.

Hitching up!

An appropriate solution was developed by 'Intermediate Technology Transport' to be made in a number of workshops in India. The cycle trailer hitches on the back of an ordinary bicycle, costs about £38, and can be made with readily available materials and simple metal working skills. A simple adaptation creates a tanker model for transporting water and other liquids.

One purchaser of a cycle trailer is an enterprising young man called Kumblaka, who comes from a family of agricultural labourers. Some time ago, he noted that many everyday products could not be purchased in his village. He began taking his bicycle to the nearest large town and riding back home with coconuts, lentils, soap and other items in daily use, which were difficult to obtain in the villages. Using only his bicycle, Kumblaka could not carry more than 15 or 20 kg and still ride it.

The cycle trailer has proved to be an ideal investment. With a loan of 875 rupees (£38) from a local moneylender, at an interest rate of 3% a month, he was able to start carrying 100 kg of goods at a time in the trailer, and expand his trade to three other villages. He managed to pay off his loan within three months as a result of the increase in sales made possible by the trailer.

ENERGY

Tide and wave power

The tides are caused by the gravitational attraction of the moon. There are still examples in the UK of tide mills (Eling near Southampton and Woodbridge in Suffolk) where the incoming tide is trapped by a dam, and released via a water wheel or turbine at low tide. Now, there are plans, for example, to put a barrage across the estuary of the River Severn in order to generate electricity, but the bird life of the locality would be badly affected. Technologists have to take into account the effects on the environment when planning and designing such large scale works.

Another possibility is to make use of the up and down motion of the waves to generate electricity and many devices for this are being tried out. A main problem is that of getting continuous motion.

Did you know?

A tidal power station on the Rance estuary, France is able to generate 240 MW of electricity.

Wave-powered lightbuoy

Lightbuoys are used to mark navigation channels in estuaries and harbour entrances. They need to continue to work with a minimum of maintenance. The buoy shown in the photograph has achieved this by the ingenious use of wave power.

The floating body of the buoy is attached to the sea bed by a flexible hose. As the body rises and falls in sympathy with the wave motion, the hose stretches and relaxes. This causes a pumping action. Water is forced from the top end of the hose, via a non-return valve, to drive a turbine. The spilled water is drawn back into the hose through another non-return valve.

Electrical energy from the generator is fed into a charger unit for storage batteries. These batteries provide a continuous source of energy to the navigation lights, regardless of the state of the sea.

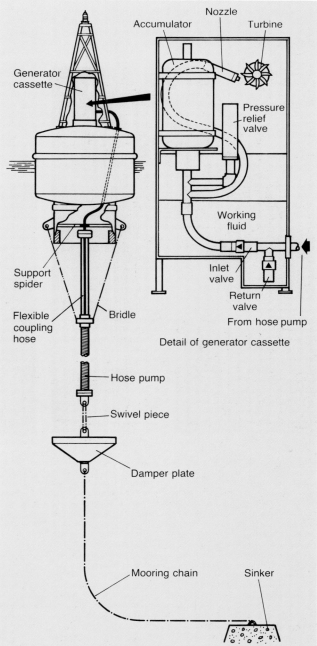

Detail of generator cassette

SYSTEMS

Crossing a river   *One problem; many solutions*

1

2

3

Solution 1
Go through it! Why is there a depth marker which shows up to five feet (1.5 metres)?

Solution 2
Build arches on arches. This Roman aqueduct in Southern France was built to carry drinking water over the valley of the River Gard to the city of Nimes.

Solution 3
Span with steel girders. This temporary 'Bailey' bridge makes use of the strength of steel in both tension and compression.

Solution 4
Construct a trestle bridge with readily available timber. The photo is of a modern concrete version of an old wooden tramway bridge.

Solution 5
Float across on a ferry. What do you think the chain (right foreground) is for?

Solution 6
Use the arch principle with iron. Another material which is strong in compression. The Iron Bridge in Shropshire was built in 1779. Why is it held together with pegs like woodworking joints?

Solution 7
Hang it all! The deck of Chelsea Bridge is suspended from two bundles of steel cables. The cables are anchored on each side of the river in huge concrete foundations. Why are the towers supported on large hinges?

5

6

4

7

PROJECTS

Experimentation and modelling

Technological design is very much a matter of 'try it and see'. You will find that the ideas you propose for solutions will need to be tried out by making **models** or **mock-ups** in easy materials such as card, plastic sheet, modelling clay or thin copper wire. Parts of the final solution will need to be experimented with to see if they perform as required. Construction kits such as *Meccano*, *Fischer Technik* or *Lego Technic* are very useful for testing rough ideas quickly before getting involved in manufacturing from raw materials. In electronics, you may need to use **systems kits** or **prototyping breadboards** before soldering up a more permanent circuit.

Using kits ▲

◄ Mechanical prototyping kits

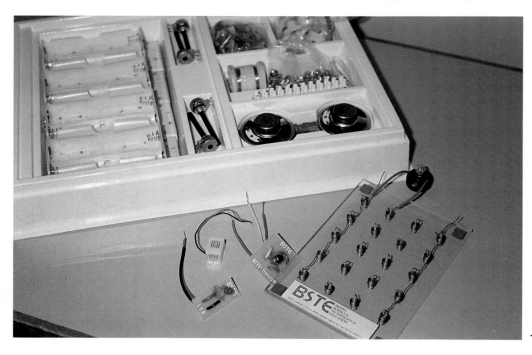

◄ Electrical and electronic kits

Communicating ideas

Communication with:	Purposes
• Self • Teacher • End user • Examiner	• Record information researched • Record and develop ideas • Plan manufacture • Record results of tests • Make evaluation

The **communication skills** necessary in project work are **talking**, **writing** and **drawing**. There are a number of technological aids which can be used to help communication, such as cameras, video systems, tape recorders, computers for word processing and graphics. Remember that all these devices need time to learn how to use them effectively. You may get better results by using what you know and can do well.

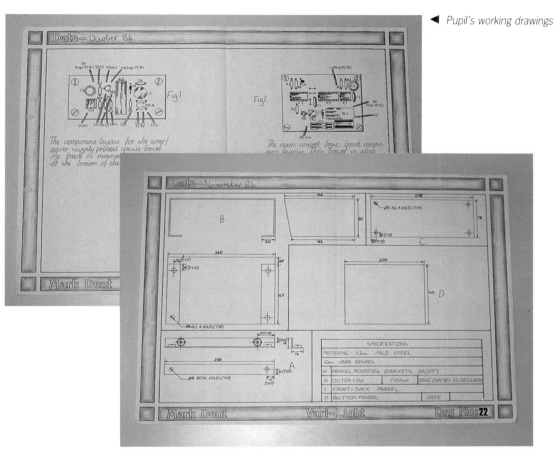

◀ Pupil's working drawings

Visualising ideas

In order to think out and develop ideas for solutions you will need to use rapid sketching techniques. Sometimes it is better to make a three-dimensional model in paper, card etc. or use a construction kit rather than a pencil drawing to visualise your ideas. A photograph of the model is useful for the final report.

The final solution will need to be communicated with sufficient detail to enable someone else to make it with very few extra instructions. Depending on the type of end product, some form of technical drawing will be necessary using standard symbols. You will find a selection of these in the data section on page 85.

(See also page 67)

▲ Computer aided graphics

PROJECTS

Project ideas

Photograph 1
The analogue signal from two thermistors had to be converted into a suitable digital form to be read by the computer. A trial circuit was built on a breadboard. Component values and connections were altered until the circuit operated satisfactorily.

Photograph 2
The circuit layout was redesigned so that it could be built on stripboard. The final circuit was tested and any soldering or wiring faults put right.

Photograph 3
A rough layout of all the parts of the system was made full-size on paper. A wooden box was made to house the parts to enable the system to be portable.

The pupil's aim for this project is given on page 64. Having looked at a number of possibilities, the use of a ZX81 computer for monitoring temperatures was decided upon.

Photograph 4
The parts were wired up and tested with the computer program running. When the system was working satisfactorily, the parts were fixed securely and the lid of the box screwed on. The whole system was put to use in the church while the heating was on and the temperatures obtained were analysed.

Project Development

6

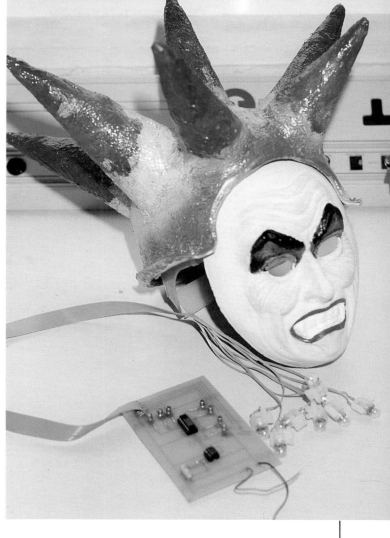

7

8

Photograph 5
These telephone dialling aids were thoroughly tested by people with
arthritic and similar conditions in their hands. The pupil's folder included
completed questionnaires which helped her to evaluate the designs.

Photograph 6
The pupil who designed this unit has aimed to allow partially-sighted
children to experience a variety of different textures, surfaces and
feelings. He visited special schools for both research and evaluation of
the project. When pressed, the buttons operate electronically-generated
sounds, and a small fan can be switched on. The shapes are secured
with Velcro. The top of the unit was vacuum formed.

Photograph 7
A special mask was needed for a school play. The mask had to have
randomly flashing lights on the ends of the 'spikes'. The solution uses
microelectronics to achieve this effect. The mask is made from glass
reinforced plastic (GRP).

Photograph 8
This plant watering device uses the logic inputs from a moisture sensor
AND a water level sensor in its tank to control a pump. When the soil is
wet the pump is switched off. The amount of water delivered is
adjustable for different plant conditions. A considerable number of
alternative methods were investigated before this particular design was
developed.

Dealing with small signals (cont. from page 47)

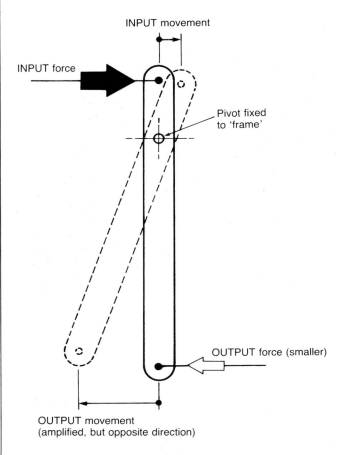

INPUT movement

INPUT force

Pivot fixed
to 'frame'

OUTPUT force (smaller)

OUTPUT movement
(amplified, but opposite direction)

◀ *Amplification by a lever*

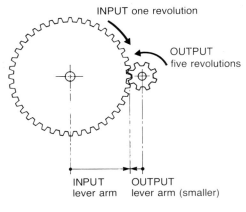

INPUT one revolution

OUTPUT
five revolutions

INPUT
lever arm

OUTPUT
lever arm (smaller)

▲ *Amplification by gearing*

Mechanical amplifiers can be used for linear and angular displacements for direct displays or for chaining other sensors.

The **diaphragm valve** is another example of an amplifier. The valve can be operated by a small input pressure signal. The large surface area of the diaphragm produces a large enough force to switch the air valve on.

▲ *A diaphragm valve*

Display devices

▲ *The human weather station!*

When a sensor is being used as part of a control system it is usually not necessary to be able to read *values* of the measurement being made. If, however, the system is designed for making measurements, for example a weather station, it is essential to have a display or record of the measurements.

Analogue or digital?

Analogue displays, such as the multimeter illustrated, show the variation of the value continuously. This has advantages if you are trying to watch the variation, although most meters will respond quite slowly and may just flicker around the average value.

Digital displays show only digits, which makes it difficult to see the extent of variations, but they are faster to read and easier for non-specialists.

Using an analogue meter

A voltmeter is connected across the two points where the measurement is required (i.e. **in parallel** with the components). In electronics it is usual to make measurements relative to 0 volts (normally the negative terminal of the power supply).

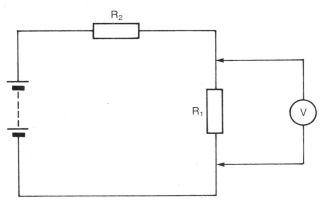

▲ *Using a voltmeter to find the voltage across R_1. This will not be the battery voltage because there is a voltage drop across R_2.*

▲ *Digital (left) and analogue (right) meters*

To measure the current flow through a wire or component, an ammeter is inserted in the circuit (i.e. **in series** with the component).

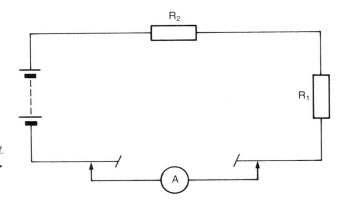

Using an ammeter to find the current flowing in a circuit. The same current flows through R_1 and R_2 ▶

Activity

Connect a 1.5 volt dry battery to a 10 kΩ (10 000 ohm) potentiometer as in the diagram. Attach a 3 volt full-scale-deflection analogue meter and a digital meter (set to at least 3 volts) to the points shown. Vary the potentiometer position slowly, and quickly, and watch the two meters. How do they respond to the changes of voltage?

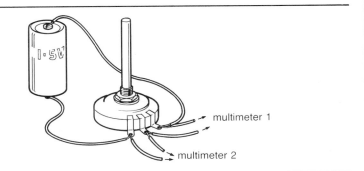

multimeter 1

multimeter 2

Digital measurements

Any sensor which has a simple switching action can be easily connected to a computer user port interface, and the inputs counted or timed. **Software** is available to count or time to the nearest millisecond (e.g. CONTROL BASIC from 'RESOURCE').

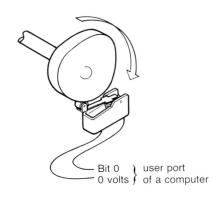

Bit 0 } user port
0 volts } of a computer

▲ *Cam operated microswitch*

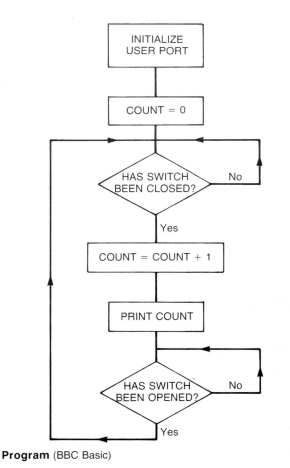

INITIALIZE USER PORT

COUNT = 0

HAS SWITCH BEEN CLOSED? — No

Yes

COUNT = COUNT + 1

PRINT COUNT

HAS SWITCH BEEN OPENED? — No

Yes

Program (BBC Basic)

```
10  ?65122=1          50  IF N=?65120 THEN 50
20  N=?65120          60  C=C+1
30  C=0               70  PRINT C
40  REPEAT            80  IF N<>?65120 THEN 80
                      90  UNTIL FALSE
```

Timing loop flow chart ▶   Note: Switch may need to be debounced by a Schmitt trigger IC

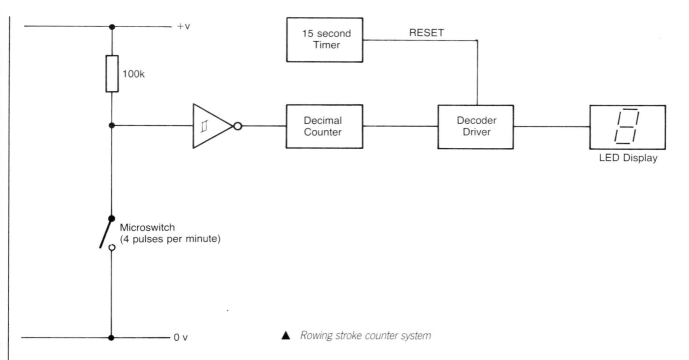

▲ *Rowing stroke counter system*

Counting can be done by integrated circuits. If the input sensor is a switch it must be **debounced** to prevent extra pulses being counted.

Using resistance-type sensors

Resistance sensors include thermistors, light dependent resistors and potentiometers. They are analogue sensors, that is their value of resistance can vary. A direct reading of resistance can be made with an ohmmeter. The resistance can be put in series with another resistor to make a **potential divider** as in the diagram.

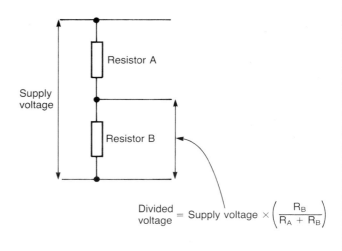

A potential divider ▶

$$\text{Divided voltage} = \text{Supply voltage} \times \left(\frac{R_B}{R_A + R_B}\right)$$

If a project needs a particular value of the resistance of the sensor to switch on a device, then a **transistor switch** can be used. An example of this would be a porch light which is to be switched on at dusk.

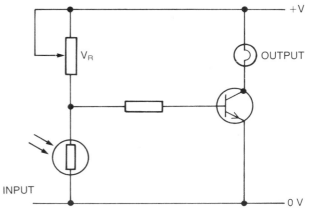

A transistor switch ▶

As it gets dark, the resistance of the LDR will increase. The divided voltage will therefore increase sufficiently to switch the transistor on.

The variable resistor V_R is used to set the level at which switching occurs. The supply voltage depends on the output lamp used, and the type of transistor.

SENSING AND MEASURING

The voltage across one resistor of a potential divider can be 'read' by a voltmeter or the analogue port of a BBC computer.

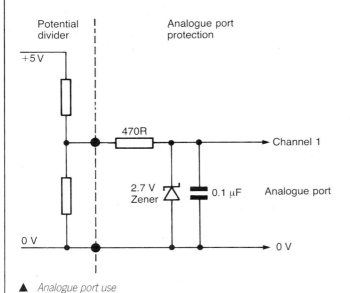

▲ *Analogue port use*

The analogue port is read by **PRINT ADVAL(C)** where 'C' is the channel number (1, 2, 3 or 4) being used. Up to four sensors can be read in this way. The ADVAL number obtained varies from 0 to 65536 and is best divided by 16 to give more easily used numbers in a program. The input from sensors can be used in a control program.

Variations with time

Variations of voltage, such as the signal from an **astable multivibrator** (e.g. 555 timer) or timing circuit, are best observed using an oscilloscope. Connect the output of your circuit to the Y input and adjust the 'volts/div' and 'time/div' dials until your signal is on the screen clearly.

▲ *An oscilloscope*

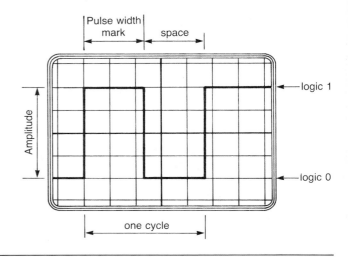

A typical oscilloscope trace of a square wave ▶

Photoelasticity

A number of translucent materials such as glass, PMMA (acrylic), polystyrene, Araldite CT200 and cellulose nitrate, have the optical property of **double internal refraction** when stressed. Light is retarded in proportion to the stress. In **polarised light**, coloured fringes can be seen. The effects of loading on components can be observed by placing translucent models into a **polariser**.

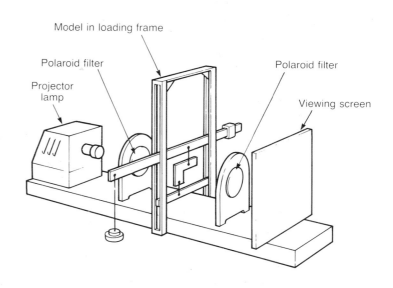

A polariscope ▶

The **fringe pattern** shows areas of high change of stress. The effects of redesigning components (e.g. a change from sharp to rounded corners) can be clearly seen by the reduction of the number of lines in the pattern. The calculation of actual stress is more complicated.

Stress patterns on a loaded beam as seen in a polariser ▶

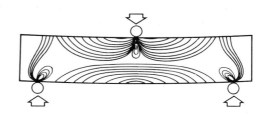

Speed and position

A number of technological projects need either speed measurement or position sensing. Here are a few ideas:

▼ *Some methods of speed measurement and/or position sensing*

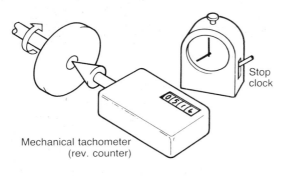

Mechanical tachometer (rev. counter)

Stop clock

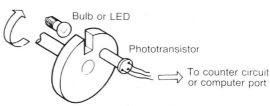

Bulb or LED

Phototransistor

To counter circuit or computer port

With several cutouts or holes this can be a position sensor

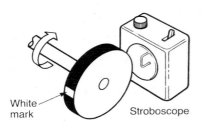

White mark

Stroboscope

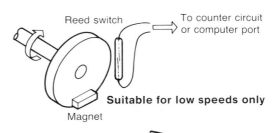

Reed switch

To counter circuit or computer port

Magnet

Suitable for low speeds only

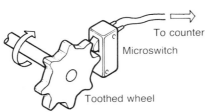

To counter

Microswitch

Toothed wheel

This can be used for speed or position

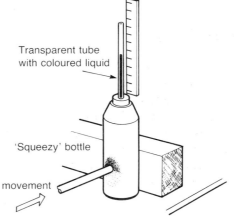

Transparent tube with coloured liquid

'Squeezy' bottle

movement

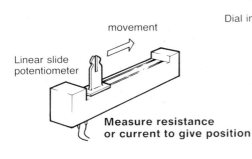

movement

Linear slide potentiometer

Measure resistance or current to give position

Dial indicator

movement

Parallel line gratings (e.g. Letratone on transparent plastic)

movement

The number of dark 'fringes' can be counted by phototransistor as the gratings move relative to each other

How accurate?

The **accuracy** of any measurement will depend on the **suitability** of the system being used and its **limitations**. It would be hopeless to try to measure the length of a component to the nearest tenth of a millimetre with an ordinary rule; a micrometer or vernier calliper would be needed. Always, you need to use the right measurement system for the job.

Errors can occur from mistakes in reading instruments or by incorrect calibration. Check your calibration before reading a result and double check your readings.

Activity

Measure the voltage of a battery with several different voltmeters. If possible, include a meter with a mirror scale. How much difference is there between readings? How accurately can you read each meter? Is there a connection between accuracy and the cost of the measuring instrument?

Test yourself on . . . . sensing and measuring

1 Identify suitable input sensors and output display devices, when measuring in these situations.
   a the angle of rotation of a surveying instrument
   b the speed of a motor
   c the number of boxes passing a point on a conveyer
   d the moisture content of soil
   e the level of light outside a house
   f the daily amount of rainfall at a particular site

2 What is the input and output of each of these sensors/transducers?
   a a loudspeaker
   b a microswitch
   c a thermocouple
   d a thermistor

3 Why is signal amplification necessary for strain gauges?

4 What are the possible sources of errors in these measurement systems?
   a the power output of a model wind generator
   b the speed of flow in a water pipe
   c the number of revolutions of a wheel

5 how can photoelasticity help in the design of structural components?

▲ *A surveying instrument in use*

▲ *Loudspeakers*

PROJECTS

Situations

A project always starts with an observation of a need. This can be your own, your family's or a general human need. You should try to look at the situation carefully, describe it in writing, sketch it and, if possible, take photographs. You will have to go back to these observations later to test your ideas and evaluate the effectiveness of your final solution.

What is the real problem?

To design more efficient windscreen wipers? No! The problem is to keep the windscreen clear so that the driver can see out. There are a number of other solutions other than wipers. For example, the surface of the windscreen (glass or..?) could be treated to make it water repellent.

Activity

For each of these 'solutions' try to write down what may have been the original problem or need.

- Refrigerator • Pianoforte • Microwave oven • Sliding doors
- Ball point pen • Overhead projector • Pressure cooker

PROJECTS

Aims

WHERE DID YOU SAY THE TARGET WAS?

Often this is because the aim was trying to cover too wide an area and solve all the world's problems in one go! Remember to record any changes and the reasons for them in your final report.

A **good aim** will be clear and precise and define the starting points and limits of the project.

Poor aims

The following are examples of **poor aims** for the reasons given.

I want to make a racing car.	There is no need stated. Why do you want a racing car? Is this full size or a model? Will you improve an existing car or design from scratch?
To design a tap holder for a disabled person.	This aim is better, but also gives a solution rather than the problem that the disabled person is experiencing. The actual designed solution could be something quite different from a tap *holder*.

It has been said that if you don't know where you are going you won't get there! With project work, it is very important to have a clear statement in writing of what you are trying to do. However, it is common for students to find that after some research and design work the original aim needs modification.

A clear aim

> The aim of this project is to be able to investigate the efficiency of the church heating system and to enable us to reduce heating costs by not having the heat on unnecessarily.
>
> I decided to use a computer in this project because it shouldn't require much electronics to make the computer read temperatures. Also it is adaptable and if necessary the computer could be made to make several copies of the temperature reading or store them on cassette tape. If a computer was not used printing the temperature values onto paper in any form would be very difficult.
>
> I decided to use a ZX81 computer because I think that this will be quite adequate for dealing with temperature measurement with extra circuitry added. I already possess a ZX81 and am able to program it.

Starting and limiting

How are you expecting your solution to **perform**? Look back at the system design factors on page 16. For each of the factors which apply to your problem, you need to write down a clear statement (**specification**) of performance.

It is a good idea to state, after the aim, the parts of the project that you will *not* be attempting, and also the assumptions you have made so that you don't have to 're-invent the wheel'.

FINAL DESIGN RELATING TO SPECIFICATION:	
IS IT WATERPROOF?	ON MY MODEL I AM PLANNING TO GLUE THE JOINTS TO KEEP IT WATERPROOF, SO THE ANSWER TO THIS QUESTION IS – YES.
IS IT ADJUSTABLE?	IT IS NOT ABLE TO BE FITTED TO ANY PART OF THE BOAT BUT IT CAN BE FIXED TO ANY TYPE OF MATERIAL, e.g. WOOD OR FIBRE GLASS.
IS IT LIGHT?	IT WEIGHS 125 GRAMS WHICH IS VERY LIGHT AND WILL NOT BE EXTRA WEIGHT FOR ROWERS TO PULL ALONG.
EASY TO USE?	IN PRACTICE IT SHOULD WORK, WITH HARDLY ANY UNDERSTANDING.
IS IT HARDWEARING?	THE PLASTIC CASE IS QUITE HARDWEARING BUT IF I WAS GOING TO USE THE MONITOR IN THE BOAT I THINK I WOULD FIND ANOTHER MATERIAL THAT IS HARDER, AND THAT WILL LAST LONGER.
IS IT PORTABLE?	IT IS NOT VERY PORTABLE EVEN THOUGH I HAVE MADE A BREAK IN THE MIDDLE OF THE WIRES LEADING TO THE MICROSWITCH SO THE MONITOR CAN BE TAKEN AWAY.

▲ *Specification for a rowing stroke counter*

Research and investigation

Once you are clear about what you want to aim at, the next job is to investigate 'how'. It may help to look at the way other people have solved the problem, but this is better done after you have some ideas of your own. There are two parts to research:
- information gathering
- experimentation on possible solutions.

Where to look

Unless the situation is very familiar to you, you will always need to find information. Sometimes it is possible to find a book from a library with just the right title! More often though, you will have to do some detective work and dig deeper. Libraries usually have a subject index, either on cards or microfilm. Most technical books will have lists of other books and magazines in them (usually called 'Bibliographies') which may help your hunt. When you find some useful information, don't copy it out word for word. Make short notes and sketches of the parts which you need. Don't forget to make a note of the name and author of the book or article for your report.

Activity ───────────────

Find out how your local or school library classifies book and non-book materials.

PROJECTS

In which sections of the library would you look to find information on 'Water Wheels'?

An extract from a library classification:

000	General	621	Mechanical Engineering
100	Philosophy	624	Civil Engineering
200	Religion	630	Agriculture; food production
300	Social Sciences	670	Manufacturing
380	Public Utilities	690	Building
386	Inland Waterways Transport	700	The Arts
400	Language	720	Architecture
500	Pure Science	728	Residences
530	Physics	800	Literature
600	Technology	900	History, Geography, Biography
620	Engineering		

Writing letters

Manufacturers' leaflets are a useful source of information. Do remember that a large number of other pupils are doing projects, and companies are very busy doing their own work! If you write asking "Have you got anything about level-crossings?", don't expect a very helpful reply! Be very precise about what you want, and include a stamped, self-addressed envelope.

St. Martin's College
Strawberry Hill

Dear Sir or Madam,
I am in my 5th year at school studying CDT Technology. As part of my coursework I am doing a project. I am interested in devising a sensor to measure the force on my shins when I do a cross-step when throwing the javelin.
I have suffered from shin splints and stress fractures and I would use such a device in some way to alter my technique by experimenting with the position in which I put my foot down when I throw, or changing my technique completely.
I would appreciate any information you could send me that would help me with my project.
I enclose a self-addressed envelope.
Yours faithfully
Alan Footman.

(See colour pages 52 and 53 for Experimentation and modelling and Communicating ideas.)

The manager,
Electronics Ltd,
Park Road,
Teddington.

Dear Sir or Madam,
I am undertaking a technology project in my final year at school. I am investigating the possibility of making an electronic spirit level, the purpose of which would be to provide a greater degree of accuracy in situations where visibility was difficult — possibly for use with the blind. It would therefore, have to indicate vertical and horizontal surfaces using sound rather than a visual display.
In order to decide whether I should pursue this project, I would appreciate any information you could send me about what is available on the market, and any suggestions that you think may be of use to me.
I would be grateful for any assistance.
Yours faithfully
Lisa Andrews.

Drawing methods

Planning

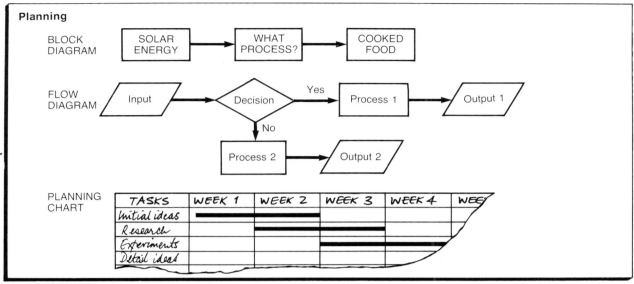

BLOCK DIAGRAM

SOLAR ENERGY → WHAT PROCESS? → COOKED FOOD

FLOW DIAGRAM

Input → Decision → Yes → Process 1 → Output 1

No → Process 2 → Output 2

PLANNING CHART

TASKS	WEEK 1	WEEK 2	WEEK 3	WEEK 4	WEE
Initial ideas	▬▬▬▬				
Research		▬▬▬			
Experiments			▬▬▬▬		
Detail ideas					

Visualising ideas

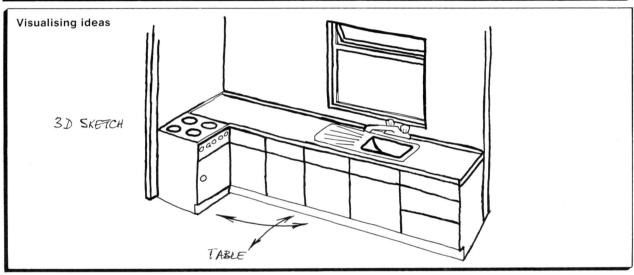

3D SKETCH

TABLE

Detailing ideas

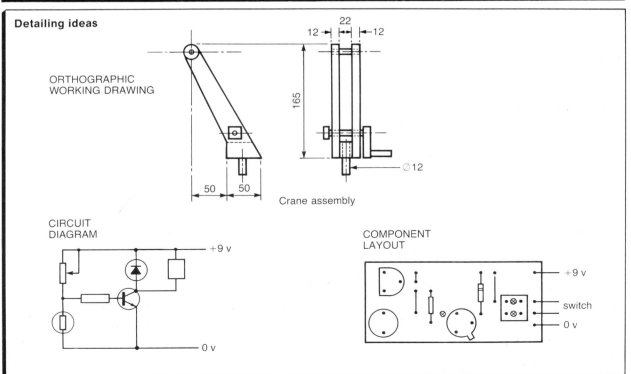

ORTHOGRAPHIC WORKING DRAWING

22
12 — 12
165
50 50
Ø12

Crane assembly

CIRCUIT DIAGRAM

+9 v

0 v

COMPONENT LAYOUT

+9 v
switch
0 v

Materials and structures

When you have some firm ideas about the possible solutions, some decisions have to be taken about the choice of materials. You may be restricted to the small range of materials available in school, or perhaps you will need to order the right piece for the job. In either case you need to know what properties are needed to make a sensible choice.

There are two aspects to take into account:
- Properties needed for manufacture — can you bend it, drill it, joint it, etc.?
- Properties needed for performance of the device — will it take the load, stand the heat, take the current, etc.?

Properties of common materials

The perfect material does not exist. Some materials have better properties for a task than others. This table will give you some idea of the relative strengths and weaknesses of materials commonly available. Engineering handbooks will give you actual tested values for these properties.

Properties of materials ▼

Property	Performance rating *** = Best * = Worst													
Resistance to tension	*	**	*	**	***	*	*	*	*	**	**	*	*	**
Resistance to compression					***				*				**	
Hardness	**		***						*					
Ease of press forming	***				**									*
Ease of heat softening				*			***	**						
Lowest rate of expansion		**					*							***
Resistance to corrosion		**			*	***								
Conductance of electricity		**		***	*									
Conductance of heat				***				*						**
Ease of magnetisation			***		**									
Material	Aluminium	Copper	Iron (cast)	Silver	Steel (mild)	Melamine	Polyethylene	Polystyrene	Balsa wood	Oak	Pine	Brick	Concrete	Glass

Activity

Devise your own tests to compare the properties of a number of different materials. Give them a rating as in the table.

Activity

Some materials perform better in service when they have some form of protective coating. Devise a series of tests to compare different coatings, such as paint, preservatives and varnish, on the weathering performance of different timbers.

Dealing with forces

What type of **stresses** might be affecting your project's structure due to external loading?

$$\text{stress} = \frac{\text{external load}}{\text{cross-sectional area}}$$

If two similar structural members are subjected to exactly the same load, the member with the larger cross-sectional area, normal to the direction in which the load is applied, will have the least stress.

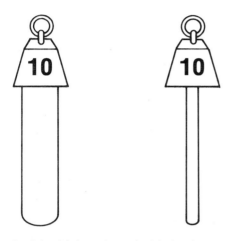

Same load, but **higher stress** in right-hand component

Tensile stresses are caused by forces **pulling** the structural member at each end.

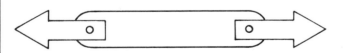

▲ *Tensile loading*

▲ *Loads placed on the hook of this crane will put the supporting cable into tension.*

WELL... I WAS TOLD TO DEAL WITH THE FORCE!!

Compressive stresses are caused by forces **pressing** the ends of the structural member together.

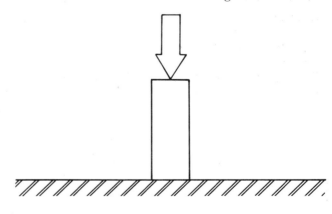

▲ *Compressive loading*

◀ *Concrete columns — an example of compressive loading*

69

Torsional stress is caused when the two ends of a structural member are **twisted** in opposite directions.

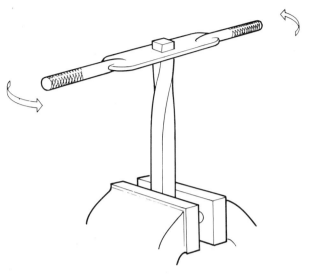

▲ Torsion loading

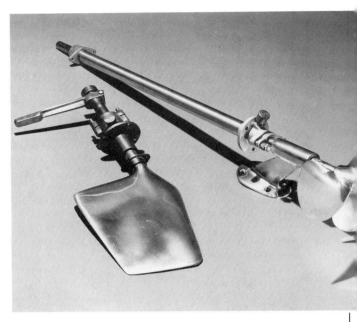

▲ The drive shaft of this propeller experiences torsional loading

Combinations of stresses

All the types of stresses illustrated above are due to **end loading** on a structural member. If **loads** are **carried along the length** of a member, such as a beam, **bending** is caused. This results from a combination of tensile, compressive and shear stresses.

Shear stress is caused when two opposing forces act together across a member.

▼ Bending stresses in a beam

Shear stress
across the section between load and supports

LOAD

Compressive stress
throughout top section

Neutral axis
(no stress)

Tensile stress
throughout lower section

SUPPORT
REACTION

SUPPORT
REACTION

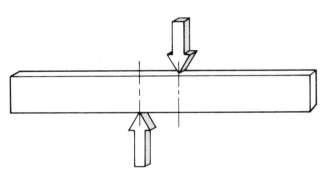

▲ Shear loading

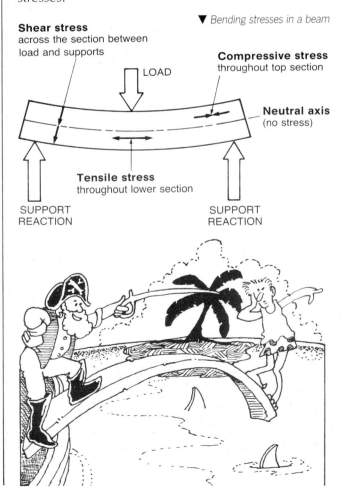

▲ A shearing cutter

Reinforcement

Some materials are very poor at resisting tensile stresses and have to be **reinforced**. Glass fibres are used to reinforce polyester resins. Steel rods are used to reinforce concrete and take the tensile stress at the bottom of the beam and the shear stress at the ends. (See page 61 for photoelastic illustration of stresses in a beam.)

Reinforcement of concrete ▶

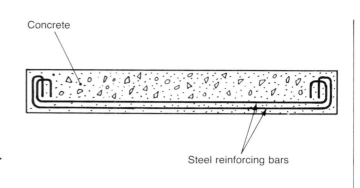

Concrete

Steel reinforcing bars

The maximum load that a beam can carry depends on the material used and also its cross-sectional shape and size. The **deeper** the beam the **less bending** there will be for a given span.

▲ *Concrete beams — a multi-storey car park under construction*

▲ *Pierced (castellated) beams to reduce weight*

Activity

Draw a grid of lines on a piece of foam block as in the photograph. Support the foam at each end and carefully load the middle. Measure the distance between the vertical lines at the top, middle and bottom of the foam, before and after loading.

What does this show?

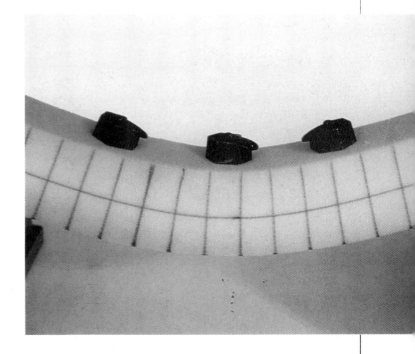

PROJECTS

Activity

Make up beams as in the drawing with sheet balsa wood or thick card. Load each of them and measure the amount of deflection at the centre. Next support them vertically and place weights on the top. What do you notice? Also twist the beams gently between your hands to see how well they resist.

Make a table of your results.

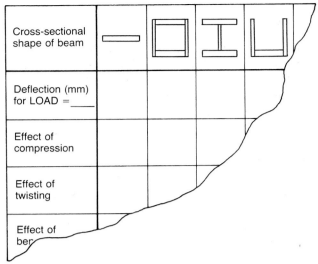

Cross-sectional shape of beam				
Deflection (mm) for LOAD =____				
Effect of compression				
Effect of twisting				
Effect of ben				

Mechanism or structure?

A structure will move until the loads are balanced by the **resistance** of the material and the **reactions** of the supports. This balancing is called **equilibrium**. If the loads cannot be balanced a structure continues to be a mechanism and in the end will collapse!

Most structural problems of stopping things moving can be tackled by putting the structure in equilibrium. The cantilever in the first drawing will fall off the support because the **turning effect** of the load is not balanced. The other drawings show some of the ways of improving the situation.

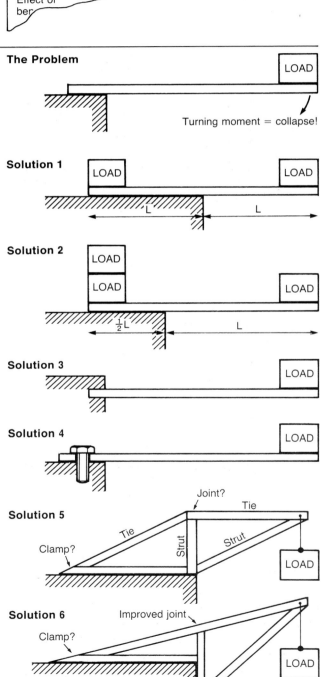

▲ *Natural cantilevers*

▲ *Designing a cantilever*

Frameworks

Triangles are **rigid** shapes. Other shapes can be made rigid by dividing them up into triangles. The members of a framework with **pin-joints** (i.e. joints which are not stiffened or reinforced) will either be in tension or in compression.

Members which resist tension are called **ties**. Those which resist compression are called **struts**. Simple frameworks can be analysed into struts and ties by inspection or by replacing a suspected tie with a piece of flexible material, such as a piece of string. Complex structures are analysed mathematically by the **resolution of forces** at each pin-joint.

▲ *A roof truss*

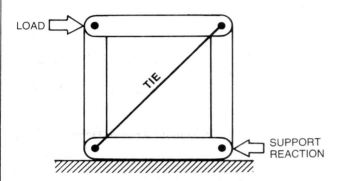

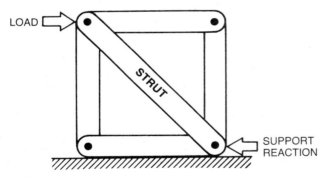

▲ *Bracing a structure!*

Activity

From a construction kit, make a four-sided shape with straight pieces of different lengths pin-jointed together (or use four cardboard strips with paper fasteners. If you disturb it, will the shape move?

Now connect a piece of cotton or string across one diagonal of the shape. What difference has this made? How could the shape be made completely rigid?

PROJECTS

Designing a structure

It is possible to get some idea of the behaviour of structures by building models. These impressions need to be backed up by calculations. Remember that a glued balsa wood bridge does not behave like the real thing! Most school projects, however, are on a fairly small scale and, provided they use the good structural principles outlined above, strength calculations are not normally needed.

▲ *Clevedon pier trestles under repair*

If calculations are essential, first the types and sizes of loads in each member have to be determined. This can often be done **graphically**. With a given shape and size of material this will give the largest value of stress to be resisted. In most structures a **factor of safety** of **at least two** is applied. This means that the working value of stress is one half of the maximum safe stress. If this value is exceeded by the loading, then either the loading must be reduced or the structure must be strengthened by increasing the size of the members.

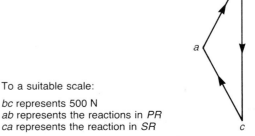

▲ *A model structure*

Find the force acting on each leg of the A-frame.

▲ *Finding forces in a particular structure*

To a suitable scale:

bc represents 500 N
ab represents the reactions in *PR*
ca represents the reaction in *SR*

Both reactions are towards *R*, therefore the loads are both compressive. Measuring *ab* or *ca* gives loads equal to 280 N in each leg.

Testing

When your final solution has been put together you will be pleased if it works at all! However, to be sure that it works properly you need to check against your statement of performance. If you didn't write one, do it now before trying to test. In testing you need to work out a means of checking the performance of your design with the standard you expected to achieve.

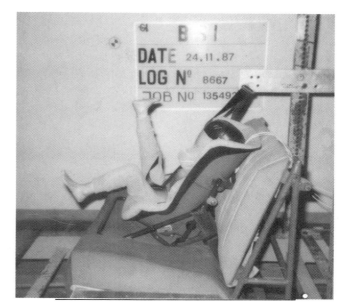

Child's safety seat being tested ▶

The manufacturer of the child's safety seat has not only made sure that the seat fits into a car and is the right size for a child, but has also tested the seat in a **simulated** crash situation. Information from this and other tests is needed before the seat can be made available for public use. For some devices there may be **legal safety requirements** which must be fulfilled.

A pupil who was investigating the shapes of cabs for lorries, has used a wind tunnel to test his models at several different wind speeds. The results from these tests will enable the pupil to decide on the best shape for further development.

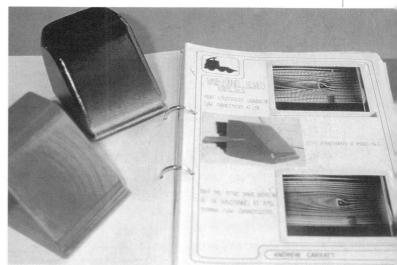

Wind tunnel tests on lorry cab models ▶

The customer is right

In many cases, designs will need to be tested by the **end users**. Make up a **questionnaire** for them to comment on the suitability of the design and how well it works for them. Be prepared for praise or criticism, and be ready to make changes to improve performance.

Example of a questionnaire ▶

PROJECT		
Automatic plant waterer	**TESTER**	
	DATE	

Where did you use the device:
In the greenhouse ☐   On houseplants ☐

When was it in use?
Holiday times ☐   Weekends ☐   All the time ☐

How well did it work?
Just right ☐   Too wet ☐   Too dry ☐

Are the control easy to   (a) understand?   YES/NO
                  (b) operate?   YES/NO

What improvements do you think are needed?

Thank you for your time and interest.

PROJECTS

Evaluation

How well does your solution match up to the original requirements of the aim? It may well be several months since the project started, so you need to look back at what was written. Your evaluation should include statements on:

- how closely the final solution fits the original aim
- the results of testing
- the opinions of the end users
- your own criticism of the final solution — areas of the design and making which could have been improved
- possible further developments of your ideas
- what you have learned for yourself.

If your final solution did not work as a whole, evaluate the parts that do work. Don't blame yourself for lack of skills or knowledge at this stage. Maybe the project turned out to be very complex and you have only managed to tackle part of the problem. Remember that your teachers and examiners are looking for **quality of thinking** and **designing skills** and not just quantity.

▼ *Pupils' evaluation sheets*

Evaluation of Performance

1). One of the first important aspects evident from testing is the pump's over keenness! Some sort of simple restrictor would be quite useful, or even a narrow delivery tube would do the trick.

2). Although there was nothing essentially wrong with the sensor, they could have been made more sensitive with little effort, i.e.: the copper plated lines could have been made a little bit closer to each other: ▯▯▯ etc.

3). The quantity of plants which the device was able to water at the same time was not particularly impressive. This could have been improved by complicating the circuit a bit more and having more plant sensors, or more simply having sub delivery tubes linked to the main one:
The disadvantage of this however would be that all the plants would have to have the same water requirements as only one sensor would be placed in a flower pot.

PLANT WATERER   DELIVERY TUBE
ONLY SENSOR   SUB TUBES

4). The plant waterer is not effective with distilled or very soft water; this is however not a great problem because most water is hard enough (especially in London) and even if the water is too soft, a small amount of $NaCl$ could be added to rectify the problem.

5). The device is not lime scale proof, but again this is no drastic problem as it would be likely to collect in the tubes which are not very expensive to replace.

TECH PROJECT		
KATHERINE VAZIRI		SR
PAGE NO.	51	
TOTAL NO. PAGES		54

SPECIFICATION

WATERPROOF: WHILE ROWING YOU ENCOUNTER WATER, SO TO KEEP IT SAFE IT MUST BE WATERPROOF.

ADJUSTABLE: WITHIN THE BOAT - IT MUST BE ABLE TO BE FITTED TO ANY PART; IT MUST BE ABLE TO BE FIXED TO A VARIOUS AMOUNT OF MATERIALS.

LIGHT: MORE WEIGHT CARRIED IN THE BOAT WILL SLOW IT DOWN, SO FOR THE BEST RESULTS IT NEEDS TO BE LIGHT.

SMALL: SO IT DOES NOT OBSTRUCT THE ROWER OR COX.

EASY TO USE: SO THAT ALL AGES CAN UNDERSTAND AND USE TO THEIR BEST ABILITY.

HARDWEARING: IT WILL BE USED FOR A LONG TIME, NEARLY EVERY DAY, 5 OR 6 TIMES PER WEEK AND ANYTHING UP TO 2 HOURS PER TIME.

PORTABLE: SO THAT IT CAN BE TAKEN AWAY BETWEEN OUTINGS.

Writing a report

The purpose of a **project report** is to communicate to your teacher and examiner (and possibly to an employer at an interview!) all the aspects of your work. The **presentation** needs to look good and clean. A wordprocessor can be used to present the written material, but your own handwriting is more personal. Check the spelling of technical words in a dictionary. Drawings need to be neat, and labelled and coloured where necessary to make them clearer. Don't overdo the colour. Use it as a **communication aid**. Rough work can often be cut out and stuck neatly on a clean presentation sheet. Check your examination syllabus for the size of folder allowed.

Essential contents

The manner of presentation may vary but there are essential aspects which should appear in all project reports:

- title of project and your name and candidate number
- a list of the contents
- the brief – details of the situation and aim of the project
- analysis of performance or specification

▲ *We have the technology!*

- research and investigation – sources found and experiments done
- development of ideas and solutions – your sketches and notes
- a plan for manufacture – details of time and materials and final working drawings
- tests carried out and their results
- evaluation – criticisms, possible improvements and further developments.

PLAN FOR MAKING

ACTION ORDER	STAGE DETAIL	TIME (HOURS) NEEDED	TIME (HOURS) ACTUAL
	Build breadboard circuit	3	2½
1	Test circuit	½	1
2	Design PCB.	1	1¼
3	Make PcB	1	1
4	Solder components	2	
5	Test PCB		
6	Make microswitch Unit		
7	Test with cam		
8			
9	Ch		

MATERIALS LIST

ITEM NO.	DESCRIPTION	MATERIAL/ TYPE	NO. REQD.	SIZE/ VALUE	SUPPLIER
1	Microswitch	Roller SPDT	1	20 mm	R.S. Comps
2	PCB	Photo-resist	1	160 x 100 mm	Rapid Electr.
3	Resistor	5%	2	10K	" "
4	Transistor	BC108	3	–	Maplin
5	Cam	Brass sheet	1	030x 3mm	School
6	Cover	Clear Acrylic	1	200x9 x 4mm	"
7	Hinge	Brass	2	25 x 10	Local shop.
			3	10 mm Dia.	Pie Eng.

▲ *Examples of a planning sheet and materials list*

PROJECTS

Project situations

These project suggestions are given as needs or questions to consider rather than solutions to follow. After defining your own aim, it's your task to research the problem and come up with your own ideas for solutions! There are many other possible starting points for projects. It's much better if you follow-up something in which you are interested and have recognised as needing a solution.

The environment

- What might be needed to help blind people tend their gardens?
- How can the partially sighted manage in the kitchen with weighing, timing, pouring liquids and cooking?
- How can people protect themselves against burglaries or break-ins?
- How could a deaf person know that there is someone at the door or that the telephone is ringing?
- How could the temperature and humidity of a room be controlled?
- How can you avoid losing greenhouse plants during frosty weather?
- What can be done about over-use of the countryside?
- Can life be made easier for people who have to use wheelchairs?
- How much water does a plant need for maximum growth?

Leisure and sport

- What effect does running have on the legs? Does the type of shoe make any difference?
- How quickly can a runner start after the starting pistol is fired?
- How much exercise does a healthy person need?
- How can you measure the stroke rate of a rowing boat?
- Is there a way of indicating when noise levels are unsafe for an individual?
- How can musicians tell how fast to play?
- Can simple theatre lighting be more effectively controlled?
- How can sailors know the strength and direction of the wind?
- Can rock climbers and mountaineers be helped by weather forecasts?

Transport and transport communications

- Can motorway congestion be avoided?
- Can rail–road level crossings be made safer?
- Can the flow of traffic into a car park be regulated?
- Can travel on public transport be made easier?
- How could road and rail transport systems be integrated in your area?

Food and health

- Can anything be done to avoid food poisoning, when the bacteria cannot be seen?
- Is there a 'normal' pulse and breathing rate?
- How can children be protected from accidents in the home?
- Can solar energy be used for cooking?
- Can food plants give more than one crop per year?
- Could elderly people be helped with the regular dosing of medicines?
- Could any ordinary bicycle double up as an exercise bike?

Education

- Can computers help young or handicapped children to learn skills?
- Are there better ways of instructing computers than by using keyboards?
- Can people be taught to recognise musical notes?
- Could there be an alternative to the printed text book?

Manufacturing Industry

Having decided on a particular branch of industry that interests you:

- How can the quality of products be tested?
- How could the size or weight of items be checked automatically?
- How could computer graphics help the small manufacturer?

(See also pages 54 and 55 for Project ideas and Project development.)

Test yourself on . . . . project work

1 Rewrite these aims to improve them.
  a To make an exercise bench
  b Pouring liquids is difficult for the blind
  c I'm going to make a hovercraft
  d Burglar alarm circuit
  e To investigate the water requirements of plants

2 Where might you find information about the following:
  a sailing equipment
  b blind children
  c model railway signalling
  d watering plants
  e theatre lighting?

3 What drawing system could be used for the following:
  a an electronic timing circuit
  b planning the manufacture of metal and plastics parts
  c the layout of a experimental low energy house
  d planning a control sequence for a model vehicle
  e showing how the parts of a wind generator fit together?

4 This is a extract from the evaluation of a student's project. Suggest what further work might be done to improve the solution.

5 Suggest the properties required and suitable materials for making the following.
  a a tray for snack meals
  b a model boat hull
  c the frame of a bed
  d the support for a TV aerial

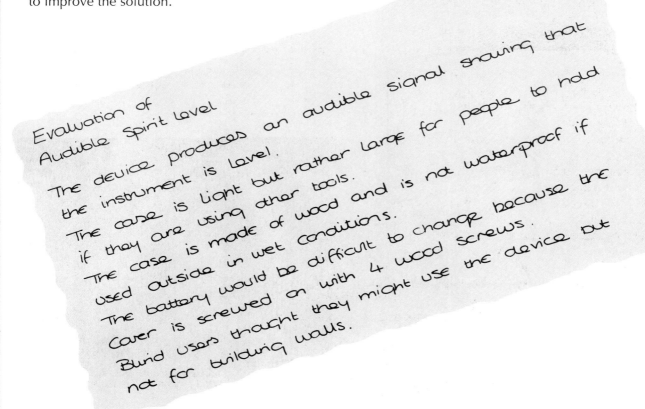

Evaluation of Audible Spirit Level

The device produces an audible signal showing that the instrument is level.
The case is light but rather large for people to hold if they are using other tools.
The case is made of wood and is not waterproof if used outside in wet conditions.
The battery would be difficult to change because the cover is screwed on with 4 wood screws.
Blind users thought they might use the device but not for building walls.

PROJECTS

6 Identify the types of stresses present in the labelled members of these structures.

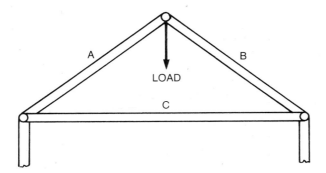

Roof truss

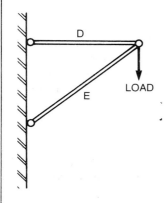

Shop sign

Lean-to roof covered in snow

7 The structures in these diagrams have weaknesses. Show how they could be improved.

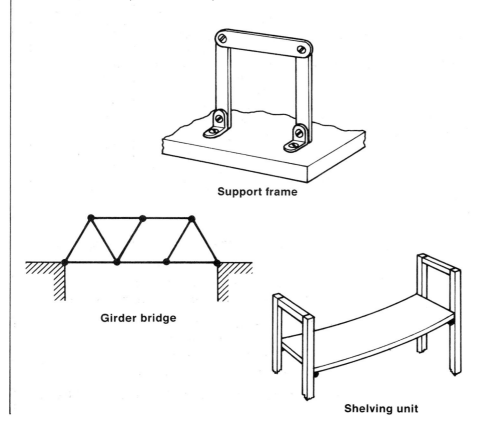

Support frame

Girder bridge

Shelving unit

USEFUL DATA

Units

All SI (Système International) or metric units can have prefix letters in front of them to indicate fractions and multiples of ten. For example, mm stands for millimetres i.e. thousandths of a metre.

Prefix	Letter	Value (powers of ten)	Value (decimal fractions)
pico	p	10^{-12}	0.000 000 000 001
nano	n	10^{-9}	0.000 000 001
micro	μ	10^{-6}	0.000 001
milli	m	10^{-3}	0.001
kilo	k	10^{3}	1000
Mega	M	10^{6}	1 000 000
Giga	G	10^{9}	1 000 000 000
Terra	T	10^{12}	1 000 000 000 000

Energy

Units

joule (J)
kilowatt hours (1 kWh = 3 600 000 joules)
A one kilowatt electric fire on continuously for one hour uses 1 kWh.

Fuel values

Energy values for solid and liquid fuels are usually expressed in megajoules per tonne (MJ/T).
(1 MJ = 1 million joules.)

Fuel	Energy (MJ/T)
Coal	26 500
Anthracite	33 300
Liquid petroleum gas	49 600
Petrol	46 900
Derv	45 600
Fuel oil	43 400

Natural gas has energy value 37.8 MJ per cubic metre.

Energy converter efficiencies

Device	Efficiency % (approximate)
Filament lamp	5
Steam locomotive	8
Solar cell	10
Fluorescent lamp	20
Internal combustion engine	25
Gas turbine	34
Nuclear reactor	39
Steam turbine	46
Hydrogen-oxygen fuel cell	60
Lead-acid battery	72
Dry cell battery	90
Hydraulic turbine	92
Electric motor	93
Electric generator	98

Note that a heat device cannot be more than about 75% efficient as there must be a temperature difference between it and the surroundings. Note also that modern materials cannot work at more than about 1100°C.

Insulation

The U value gives a measure of the insulating property of a material. It is measured in watts per square metre, degree Celsius difference in temperature. The lower the U value the better the insulator.

Material	U value $\left(\dfrac{W}{m^2 \, °C}\right)$
Solid brick 225 mm thick	2.17
Cavity wall: brick + breeze block	1.37
Cavity wall: brick + 50 mm insulated cavity + 100 mm block + 12 mm plaster	0.43
Flat roof: 3 layers felt + chipboard + joists + plasterboard	1.05
30° pitched roof: tiles + felt + 100 mm insulation	0.33
Plain wooden floor on joists	0.60
Solid floor on earth	0.56
Single-glazed window	5.6
Double-glazed window: 20 mm gap	2.9

Calculating heat loss

Taking Area to be the area of the barrier (e.g. wall or window):

Heat loss per second (watts) =
Area x U value x temperature difference

Example: Single-glazed window,
size 2.5 x 2.0 metres.
Outside temperature −1°C,
inside temperature 21°C.

Heat loss per second = 2.5 x 2.0 x 5.6 x 22 = 616 watts

Energy calculations

Work done = Force × Distance
(joules)   (newtons)   (metres)

Lifting a 10 newton weight from 0 metres to 2 metres high does 20 joules of work.

Potential energy gained by lifting =
(joules)

Mass × Gravitational field strength × height
(kg)   (10 newtons/kg)   (metres)

Kinetic energy of a moving mass =
(joules)

$\frac{1}{2}$ × Mass × Speed^2
(kg)   (metres per second)^2

Heat energy =
(joules)

Specific Heat capacity × Mass × Temperature
$\left(\frac{\text{joules}}{\text{kg °C}}\right)$ (kg)   change
(°C)

Electrical energy =
(joules)

Current × Voltage × Time
(amps)   (volts)   (seconds)

Power = Rate of doing work or
(watts)   Amount of energy used per second
(joules/second)

Structures

Stress (pascals) =
Load/Cross-sectional Area (newtons/m^2)

Strain (no units) =
Extension/Original Length (metres/metres)

Young's Modulus (E) (pascals) =
Stress/Strain (newtons/m^2)

▼ *Properties of materials*

METAL	Density kg m^{-3}	Melting point °C	Resistivity Ω m × 10^{-8}	Tensile strength M Pa	Young's modulus G Pa	NON-METAL	Density kg m^{-3}	Melting point °C	Tensile strength M Pa	Young's modulus G Pa
Aluminium	2710	660	3	80	70	Bone	1850	–	140	28
Brass	8500	1030	8	500	100	Carbon (graphite)	2300	3530		200
Copper	8930	1083	2	150	120	Concrete	2400	–	4	14
Gold	19 300	1065	2.5	120	70	Glass	2600	1130	100	70
Iron (cast)	7150	1230	10	100	110	PMMA (Perspex)	1190	180	50	3
Lead	11 340	330	21	15	20	Polyethylene	920	150	13	0.18
Silver	10500	955	1.5	150	70	Polystyrene	1050	250	50	3.1
Solder (soft)	9000	215		45		PVC (rigid)	1700	210	60	2.8
Steel (mild)	7860	1425	15	460	210	Rubber	910	30	17	0.02
Tin	7300	230	11	30	40	Wood (spruce)	600	–	7	14

Figures are approximate and depend on the actual composition of the material and its temperature

Simply supported beams

Simply supported beams

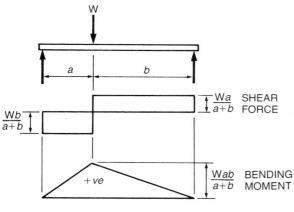

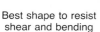

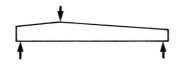

Cantilevers

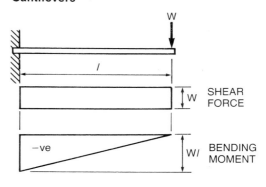

Best shape to resist
shear and bending

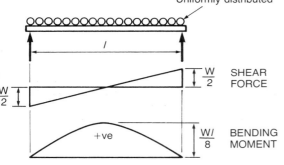

Best shape to resist
shear and bending

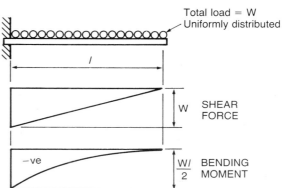

Note: Maximum bending occurs where the bending moment is greatest value.
For effect of cross-sectional shape, see page 72.

Plain frameworks

A Warren Girder made up of equilateral triangles

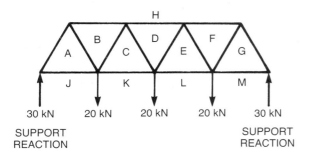

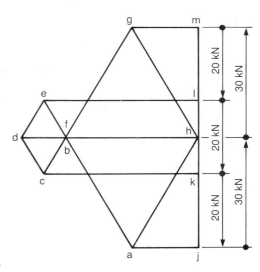

Lines on the force diagram are drawn parallel to girder members.

Lengths of these lines are measured and scaled to give the force in each member.

If the maximum safe stress is known for the material being used, the cross-sectional area and size of the members can be determined.

Example:
Sloping member far left-hand end (between spaces H and A) has a load of 34.5 kN (length ha) and is in compression. Maximum load of 46 kN is in centre top horizontal member.

Electricity

potential difference =
    (volts)

Current × resistance   (Ohm's Law)
(amps)   (ohms)

power = current × potential difference
(watts)   (amps)   (volts)

        =   current^2 × resistance
           (amps)^2 (ohms)

Resistor colour codes (4 bands)

Band	1 Figure	2 Figure	3 Multiplier	4 Tolerance
Black	0	0	× 1	Silver ±10%
Brown	1	1	× 10	Gold ±5%
Red	2	2	× 100	
Orange	3	3	× 1000	
Yellow	4	4	× 10 000	
Green	5	5	× 100 000	
Blue	6	6	× 1 000 000	
Violet	7	7		
Grey	8	8		
White	9	9		

Examples:
  Brown, Black, Red = 1 0 x100 = 1000 = 1 k ohm
       (This is sometimes written as 1k0)
  Green, Blue, Yellow = 5 6 x10 000 = 560 000
                        = 560k ohm

Resistor preferred values

Because of the tolerance, not all values are needed. A 1 kΩ resistor with ±10% tolerance (silver band) could have an actual value between −10% (= 900 Ω) and +10% (= 1.1 kΩ), so there is no need for a 900 Ω or a 1.1 kΩ resistor.

  The preferred values in the table can be multiplied by 10, 100, etc. for higher values.

E12 series (10%)	10 12 15 18 22 27 33 39 47 56 68 82
E24 series (5%)	10 11 12 13 15 16 18 20 22 24 27 30 33 36 39 43 47 51 56 62 68 75 82 91

Capacitor codes

Capacitor code numbers and the preferred values for ±20% tolerance are shown in the table.

The tolerance codes are F = ±1%   G = ±2%
J = ±5%   M = ±20%

pF (10^{-6} μF)	nF (10^{-3} μF)	μF (10^{-6} farads)	Code number
1000	1	0.001	102
1500	1.5	0.0015	152
2200	2.2	0.0022	222
3300	3.3	0.0033	332
4700	4.7	0.0047	472
6800	6.8	0.0068	682
10 000	10	0.01	103
15 000	15	0.015	153
22 000	22	0.022	223
33 000	33	0.033	333
47 000	47	0.047	473
68 000	68	0.068	683
100 000	100	0.1	104
150 000	150	0.15	154
220 000	220	0.22	224
330 000	330	0.33	334
470 000	470	0.47	474

Transistors

The letter after small signal transistor types (e.g. BC109) indicates the current gain range (h_{FE}).
A = h_{FE} of 125 − 260   B = h_{FE} of 240 − 500
C = h_{FE} of 450 − 900

The current gain is the ratio of base current to collector current i.e. $h_{FE} = I_b / I_c$

Electrical and electronic symbols

Description	BSI symbol	Common alternative (used in this book)
Variability / Pre-set adjustment		
Primary or secondary cell		
Battery of primary or secondary cells		
Alternative symbol		
Earth or ground		
Signal lamp, general symbol		
Electric bell		
Electric buzzer		
Crossing of conductors with no electrical connection		
Junction of conductors		
Double junction of conductors		
Semiconductor diode, general symbol		
Photodiode		
Light-emitting diode, LED		
PNP transistor		
NPN transistor with collector connected to envelope		
Amplifier, simplified form		

Description	BSI symbol	Common alternative (used in this book)
Transformer with magnetic core		
Ammeter		
Voltmeter		
Oscilloscope		
Motor		
Generator		
Microphone		
Loudspeaker		
Fuse		
Resistor, general symbol		
Variable resistor		
Resistor with sliding contact		
Light dependent resistor		
Capacitor, general symbol		
Polarized capacitor		
Relay		

USEFUL DATA

Common integrated circuit devices

Pin connections

74 series TTL   **40 series CMOS (Buffered)**

Logic devices with four gates each with two inputs:

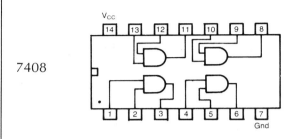

7408   AND   4081B

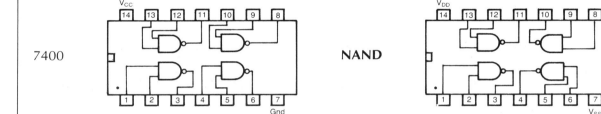

7400   NAND   4011B

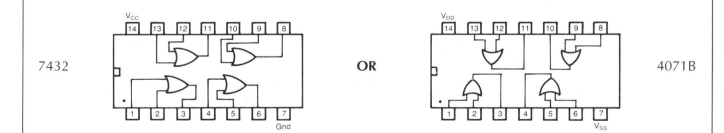

7432   OR   4071B

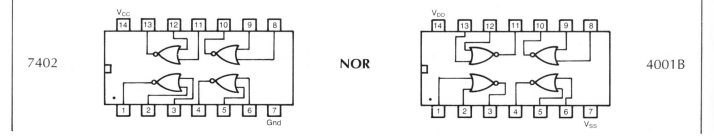

7402   NOR   4001B

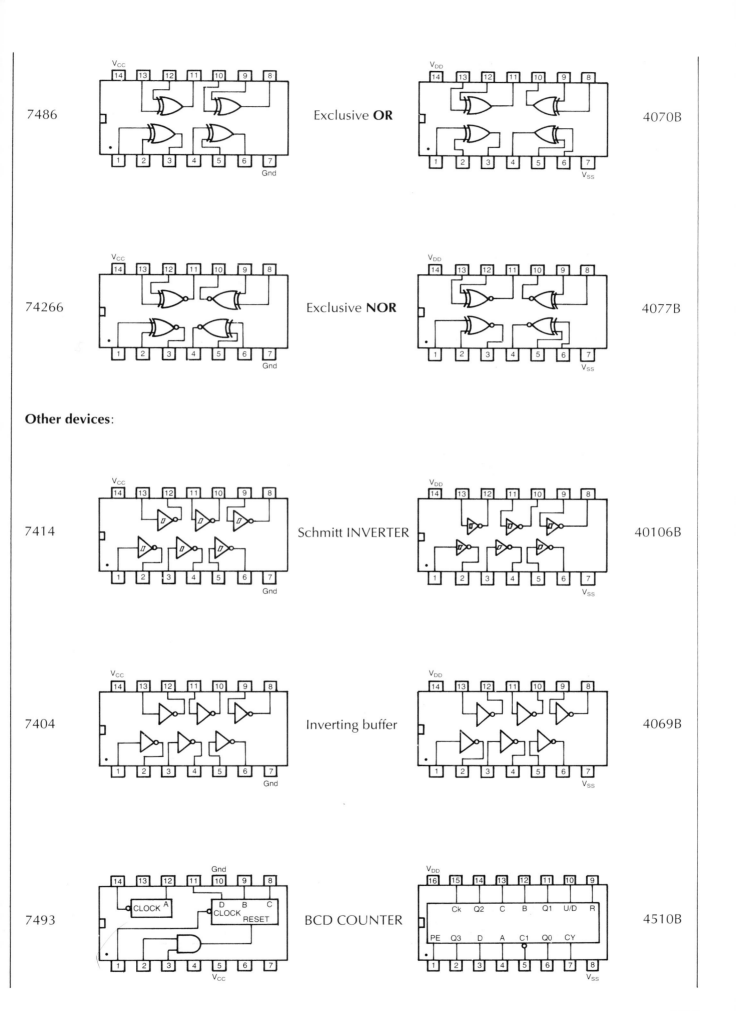

7486   Exclusive **OR**   4070B

74266   Exclusive **NOR**   4077B

Other devices:

7414   Schmitt INVERTER   40106B

7404   Inverting buffer   4069B

7493   BCD COUNTER   4510B

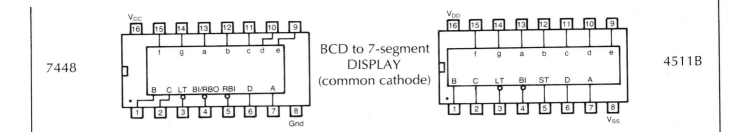

7448

BCD to 7-segment
DISPLAY
(common cathode)

4511B

BCD = Binary Coded Decimal (4 binary lines)

Operational amplifiers (e.g. 741, 081, 7611)

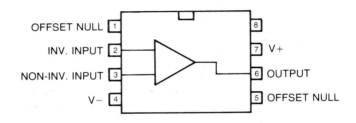

OFFSET NULL 1
INV. INPUT 2
NON-INV. INPUT 3
V− 4
8
7 V+
6 OUTPUT
5 OFFSET NULL

Timer 555

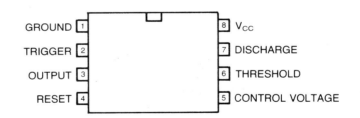

GROUND 1
TRIGGER 2
OUTPUT 3
RESET 4
8 V$_{CC}$
7 DISCHARGE
6 THRESHOLD
5 CONTROL VOLTAGE

Voltage regulators (*pin up views*)

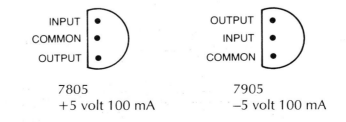

INPUT
COMMON
OUTPUT

OUTPUT
INPUT
COMMON

7805
+5 volt 100 mA

7905
−5 volt 100 mA

Typical sensors

Position

Microswitch

Contact rating typical 5 A
Mechanical life >10 M
Travel 0.5 mm
Force needed 100 − 200 g

Reed switch

Max. current 0.5 A
Max. load 15 W
Operate time 1 ms
Magnet distance 11 mm

Opto-switch slotted

Diode 1.7 V at 20 mA
Transistor 10 mA with 5 V supply

reflective

Diode 1.8 V at 40 mA
Transistor 40 mA
Distance from surface 5 mm

Float switch

Max. current 1A
Max. power 15 W
Operate min. 5°
Release max. 45°
Max. torque 2 N m

Displacement

Linear slide potentiometer

Slide length 55 mm

Rotary single potentiometer

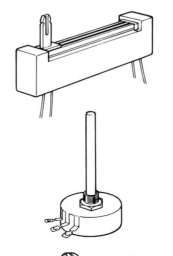

Rotation 270°

multiturn potentiometer

Rotation 10° turn

Strain gauge

Resistance 120 Ω
Gauge length 8 mm
Strain max. 4%

USEFUL DATA

Temperature

Thermostat

Bi-metal type
Range 0°C to 30°C
Differential 2°C
Switch current 16 A

Thermistor bead (RA53)

Resistance at
20°C   5k Ω
min.   115 Ω

Thermistor rod (VA1026)

Resistance at
20°C   400 Ω
min.   28 Ω

Light

Light dependent resistor
(ORP12)

Resistance
    dark 10 M Ω
    bright Sun 1 k Ω
Rise time 75 ms
Fall time 350 ms

Phototransistor

Current at 5 V supply
when light: 20 mA

Solar cell/panel

(See photo, page 21)

9 V at 50 mA when light
at 100 mW/cm²

Sound

Microphone

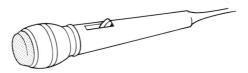

0.001 V at 1 kHz

Mechanical

$$\text{Mechanical advantage} = \frac{\text{load}}{\text{effort}}$$

$$\text{Efficiency} = \frac{\text{output work}}{\text{input work}} \times 100\%$$

$$\text{Velocity or movement ratio} = \frac{\text{distance moved by input}}{\text{distance moved by output}}$$

$$\text{Velocity ratio for spur gears (also chain and sprockets)} = \frac{\text{velocity of input gear}}{\text{velocity of output gear}}$$

$$\frac{\text{number of teeth on output gear}}{\text{number of teeth on input gear}}$$

$$\text{Velocity ratio for compound gears} = \frac{T_2}{T_1} \times \frac{T_4}{T_3}$$

$$\text{Velocity ratio for pulleys} = \frac{\text{diameter of output pulley}}{\text{diameter of input pulley}}$$

▲ *Gears from a Chinese waterpump*

▲ *Compound gearing*

USEFUL DATA

Pneumatic symbols

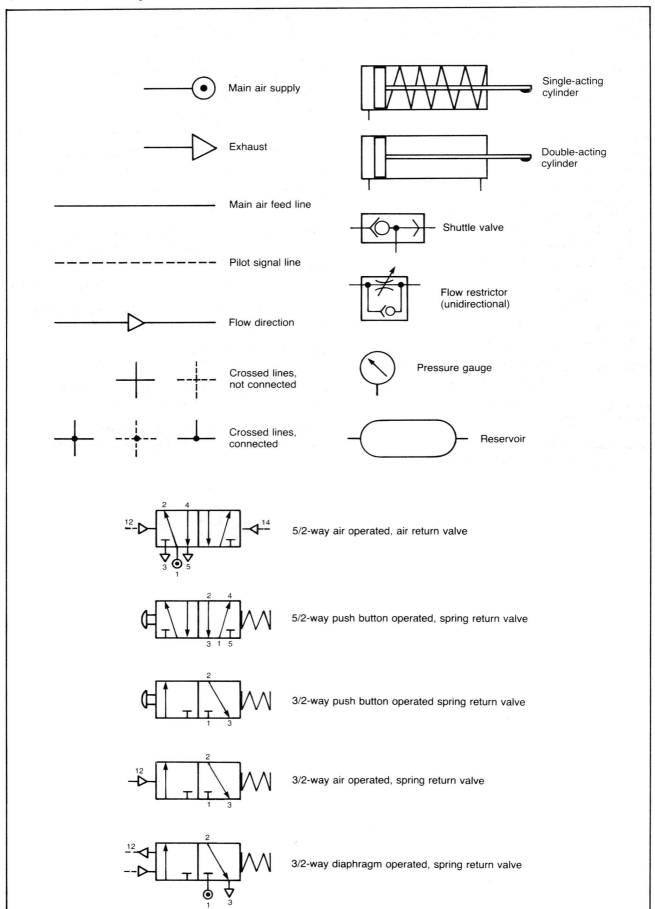

Main air supply

Exhaust

Main air feed line

Pilot signal line

Flow direction

Crossed lines, not connected

Crossed lines, connected

Single-acting cylinder

Double-acting cylinder

Shuttle valve

Flow restrictor (unidirectional)

Pressure gauge

Reservoir

5/2-way air operated, air return valve

5/2-way push button operated, spring return valve

3/2-way push button operated spring return valve

3/2-way air operated, spring return valve

3/2-way diaphragm operated, spring return valve

Useful addresses

British Industrial Biological Research Association
Woodmansterne Road, Carshalton, Surrey SM5 4DS

British Paper and Board Industries Federation
3 Plough Place, Fetter Lane, London EC4A 1AL

British Plastics Federation
5 Belgrave Square, London SW1X 8PH

British Science and Technology in Education
  (Courses and Equipment)
Carlton, Bedfordshire MK43 7LF

British Standards Institution
  BSI Sales, Linford Wood, Milton Keynes MK14 6LE
  BSI Education, 2 Park Street, London W1A 2BS

Building Research Establishment
Bucknalls Lane, Garston, Herts WD2 7JR

The Design Council
28 Haymarket, London SW1Y 4SU

Disabled Living Foundation
380-384 Harrow Road, London W9 2HU

Energy Efficiency Office, Department of Energy
Thames House South, Millbank, London SW1 4QJ

Energy Technology Support Unit
AERE Harwell, Didcot OX11 0RA

Forestry Commission
231 Corstorphine Road, Edinburgh EH12 7AT

Friends of the Earth
377 City Road, London EC1Y 1NA

Glass Manufacturers Federation
19 Portland Place, London W1N 4BH

Health and Safety Executive
  (Information and Advisory Services)
Baynards House, 1 Chepstow Place, London W2 4TP

Intermediate Technology Development Group
Myson House, Railway Terrace, Rugby CV21 3HT

International Solar Energy Society
21 Albemarle Street, London W1

National Centre for Alternative Technology
Llwyngwern Quarry, Machynlleth, Powys, Wales

RESOURCE (Computer software and hardware)
Exeter Road, Off Coventry Grove, Doncaster DN2 4PY

Trent International Centre for School Technology
Burton Street, Nottingham NG1 4BU

UK Atomic Energy Authority
11 Charles II Street, London SW1Y 4QP

Understanding Electricity, Electricity Council
30 Millbank, London SW1 4RD

The Warmer Campaign (Energy from waste)
83 Mount Ephraim, Tunbridge Wells TN4 8BS

ANSWERS TO SELF TESTS

Note
Answers to self tests are suggestions only. They are not given as complete answers or as the only possible answers.

Systems

1 (a) time set → timing → sound

(b) air and dirt → collection of dirt → clean floors/furniture

(c) wheat, grain etc → grinding → flour

(d) fuel → energy conversion → movement

(e) signal from intruder → detection → alarm signal

(f) play and directions → production → entertainment/food for thought

2

Example
Vacuum cleaner collection of dirt

→ air flow from fan → deposit dirt in bag → filter air →

electricity

3 (a) light shines → detection and switching → squeak

(b) temperature increases → level detection and device selection → fan on

sunlight gets brighter → → blind closes

(c) infra-red beam broken → switching → doors open

4 (a) Safety: no sharp edges, no toxic materials eg. paint, no small parts, non-flammable, not easily broken.

Appearance: appealing, bright colours, interesting sounds (noisy?). Value for money, teaches skills.

(b) Contents: nutritious, easy to prepare, good taste, free from artificial additives.

Package: interesting, suits people's diet ideas, describes contents.

(c) Use: simple, easy to read, few instructions.
Position: suitable for crew to read, easy to fix and remove.
Durability: not affected by knocks, bad weather or water.

(d)   Suitable for wide age range, simple rules, bright and colourful, plenty of action, durable, not easily damaged, parts contained in a box/package for storage.

Energy

1   Use gas/electricity/oil/solid fuel bills and price information. You will also need current energy values from a reference book. (See data section.)

2   Research costs at your local DIY shop or warehouse. To be cost effective the cost of materials plus installation needs to be recovered in saved energy in a reasonable number of years. Use the information from question 1 to give the cost of energy.

3 (a)   Solar panels (photovoltaic) for electricity.

  (b)   Water and wind powered turbines for electricity or direct heating from friction.

  (c)   Waste heat from power stations or from burning rubbish. Heat pumps to extract low-level heat from rivers.

  (d)   Solar panels for heating water.

Control

1 (a)   Open loop. The amount of breaking force from the rider's applied force on the brake lever is not constant. The rider 'guesses' the amount of **braking** by sensing the **deceleration**.

  (b)   Closed loop. **A** rise in temperature of the water will switch the thermostat off and switch off the heater. When the temperature drops a little the heater will come on again. The effect of heating and cooling is the feedback.

  (c)   Open loop. The sailor has to set the position of the rudder and observe the effect on the boat before making any adjustments.

  (d)   Closed loop. The revolution counter is used to feed pulses into the computer so that the distance travelled can be determined in a fixed time. The speed of the drive motors is then adjusted to give the required change.

ANSWERS TO SELF TESTS

Control

2   See 1(b) and (d).

3   Possibilities :
(i) microswitches at each end of the travel of the lens operate a bistable (relay or electronics) to reverse the motor;
(ii) the rotary motion of the motor is changed into reciprocating linear motion (eg. crank and slider). Motion is **started** and **stopped** by a switch;
(iii) a motor pinion engages with a straight rack **attached** to the lens mount;
(iv) the motor drives a long screw thread and a threaded nut is **attached** to the lens mount.

4 (a)

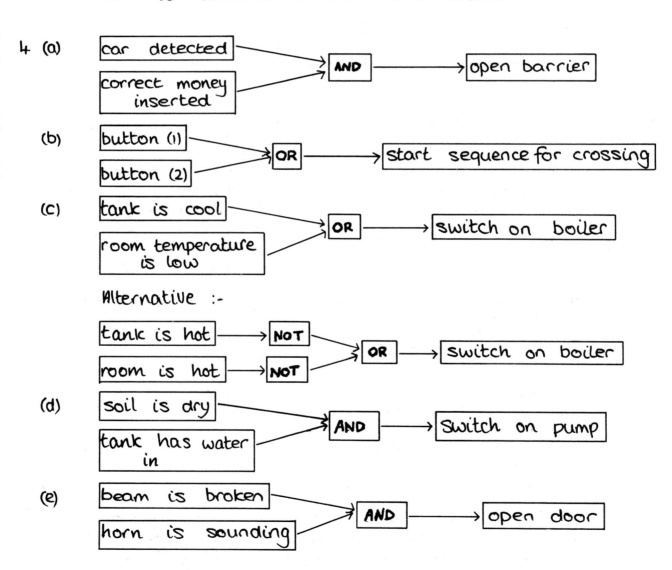

(a)
car detected
correct money inserted
→ AND → open barrier

(b)
button (1)
button (2)
→ OR → start sequence for crossing

(c)
tank is cool
room temperature is low
→ OR → switch on boiler

Alternative :-
tank is hot → NOT
room is hot → NOT
→ OR → switch on boiler

(d)
soil is dry
tank has water in
→ AND → switch on pump

(e)
beam is broken
horn is sounding
→ AND → open door

5

A	B	C
0	0	1
1	0	1
0	1	0
1	1	1

Water tank	pot	sun	pump
0	0	0	0
0	1	0	0
0	0	1	0
0	1	1	0
1	0	0	1
1	1	0	0
1	0	1	0
1	1	1	0

6   Solutions are mainly given in   CONTROL-IT/LOGO

(a)   CONTROL LOGO   ETC   BASIC

```
SWITCHON  1                 10  ?&FE62 = 1
WAIT  100                   20  ?&FE61 = 1
SWITCHOFF  1                30  FOR T = 0  TO 10000
                           40  NEXT  T
                           50  ?&FE60 = 0
```

(b)   This is best achieved by procedures for 'DASHES' and 'DOTS'.

CONTROL LOGO   procedure   'DASHES'

```
REPEAT 3
   OUTPUT 1      (SWITCHON 1)
   WAIT 6
   OUTPUT 0      (SWITCHOFF 1)
   WAIT 2
AGAIN
```

'DOTS' would be the same except less time between switching   eg. WAIT 2 . Having built the procedures they are then called up in a program.

ANSWERS TO SELF TESTS

Control

(c)

CONTROL LOGO	BASIC

```
        CONTROL LOGO              BASIC

        REPEAT                    10  ?&FE62=3
           OUTPUT 1               20  REPEAT
           OUTPUT 2               30  ?&FE60=1
        AGAIN                     40  FOR T = 0 TO 100
                                  50  NEXT T
                                  60  ?&FE60=2
                                  70  FOR T = 0 TO 100
                                  80  NEXT T
                                  90  UNTIL FALSE
```

(d) Again procedures should be used. The delay procedure could be :-

```
        REPEAT
           OUTPUT 0          (SWITCH OFF ALL)
           IF TEST 7 = 0 THEN [MSWITCH]
        AGAIN
```

The procedure MSWITCH would be :-

```
        WAIT 200
        OUTPUT 1          (SWITCH ON 1)
```

(e) Two procedures ; MFOR for forward and MREV for reverse.

To MFOR

```
        OUTPUT  1
        REPEAT
           IF TEST 7 = 0 THEN [MREV]
        AGAIN
```

To MREV

```
        OUTPUT 2
        REPEAT
           IF TEST 7 = 1 THEN [MFOR]
        AGAIN
```

(f) Main procedure waits for a train :

```
        OUTPUT 0
        REPEAT
           IF TEST 7 = 0 THEN [LIGHTS]
        AGAIN
```

Control

```
TO LIGHTS

   REPEAT 5
     OUTPUT 2
     WAIT 1
     OUTPUT 4
     WAIT 1
   AGAIN
   GATES
```

This flashes the red lights 5 times before the gates fall, and depends on position of train sensor.

```
TO GATES

   OUTPUT 1
   REPEAT
     IF TEST 6 = Ø THEN [OUTPUT Ø]
     OUTPUT 2
     WAIT 1
     OUTPUT 4
     WAIT 1
   AGAIN
```

Sensing and measuring

1 (a) Protractor with light operated counter
Moiré fringe counter (LED display)

(b) Magnet and reed switch electronic counter (LED display)
Cam and mechanical counter

(c) Light beam and LDR
Infra-red beam and photodiode

(d) Two metal electrodes, analogue meter

(e) LDR + analogue meter
Solar cell + analogue voltmeter

(f) Float gauge, Digital display/analogue meter

2

	INPUT	OUTPUT
(a)	Sound	Voltage
(b)	Movement	Switching
(c)	Heat	Voltage
(d)	Temperature	Resistance

ANSWERS TO SELF TESTS

Sensing and measuring

3   The change in resistance is very small.

4 (a)   The measurement by generator loads the model and slows the rotation thus reducing the output.

(b)   Any measurement device placed in the pipe can affect the flow.

(c)   The wheel could rotate faster than the measurement system can cope with (eg. magnet or reed switch counting revolutions — the switch needs time to close).

5   It can show up areas of high stress which can be avoided by removing sharp corners etc.

Projects

1   A good aim expresses the original need rather than a predetermined solution. These aims are suggestions, <u>not</u> right answers:

(a)   People need to exercise and train their muscles with simple apparatus which they could use in their own home.

(b)   To make a device or devices which will help blind or partially sighted people to pour hot liquids safely.

(c)   To find a means of transporting people and goods over rough ground at a specified speed.

(d)   To find a method of preventing valuable objects being stolen from private houses.

(e)   The aim as it stands implies research only. An extended aim might be:
To make an automatic watering system which will be adjustable for different types of plants and growing conditions.

2 (a)   Books on sailing, boating supplies shops (chandlers), sailing clubs and members.

(b)   Royal National Institute for the Blind, local special schools, local clubs, Social Services Departments, Citizens' Advice Bureaux.

Projects

(c) Model railway books and magazines, local and national clubs and exhibitions, Railway employees.

(d) Garden centres and nurseries, Parks Departments, amateur gardeners, books about greenhouses, indoor and garden plants, market gardeners.

(e) Theatres (young people's clubs), books, theatre lighting suppliers, theatre museums.

3 (a) Component layout schematic, circuit diagram.

(b) Flowcharts

(c) Architectural plans, perspective (cutaway) views of interior.

(d) Flow chart, computer program flow chart symbols.

(e) Orthographic views, exploded three dimensional (eg. isometric) views.

4   Investigate ways of making the device more compact and easier to hold.
Investigate other materials (eg plastics) for exterior use.
Design a simpler battery cover — possibly with a spring-clip fastening.
Investigate further uses for levelling devices.

5 (a) Ease of cleaning, hygenic, attractive self colour, does not bend under weight of plates, does not transmit heat quickly.
Example :- vacuum formed acrylic sheet.

(b) Smooth outside surface, waterproof, not difficult to make in complex shapes, not easily damaged, self coloured.
Example :- glass reinforced plastic (GRP) moulding.

(c) Resists bending, supports load of mattress and heaviest person, easily cleaned, resistant to abrasion and knocks.
Example :- softwood (pine, spruce etc.), rectangular cross section.

Projects

(d) Resists corrosion, easily fixed to roof or chimney stack, not damaged by wind loading or rain, available in different sizes.
Example :- aluminium alloy tubing.

6 (a)
A	Compressive
B	Compressive
C	Tensile
D	Tensile
E	Compressive
F	Bending
G	Compressive
H	None (load is transferred vertically to the supports).

7 <u>Support frame</u>

Depends on type of loading but needs some form of diagonal brace, either a rigid member or two diagonal 'strings'

<u>Girder bridge</u>

Needs extra member to complete triangle, otherwise it is a mechanism.
As bridge is three-dimensional it will have similar Warren girder in a parallel plane which needs to be connected.

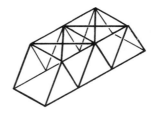

<u>Shelving unit</u>

Two problems:
(1) Vertical supports have nothing to stop them moving outwards as shelf is only supported on pegs.
(2) Shelf itself is too thin and is bending under its own weight. Either replace with thicker wood or add strips front and back.

Index